UP, DOWN, OR SIDEWAYS

PRAISE FOR *UP, DOWN, OR SIDEWAYS*

"At Zappos, one of our core training courses is built around *The Fred Factor*, so I was excited about Mark Sanborn's latest book. If you need encouragement and ideas about how to succeed during challenging times, I recommend reading *Up, Down, or Sideways*."

TONY HSIEH, *CEO of Zappos.com and* New York Times *bestselling author of* Delivering Happiness

"We all experience turbulence in our personal lives and in business, just like an airplane. Every pilot has been Up, Down, or Sideways. Mark Sanborn offers you a flight plan to prepare for and thrive in turbulent times."

HOWARD PUTNAM, *former CEO of Southwest Airlines and author of* The Winds of Turbulence

"You are holding a life-changing book—it packs a walloping prescriptive punch! Mark poignantly invites us to gain wisdom from the crucible of personal and professional setbacks and guides us to savor faith, family, and friends. Read it, and the people you care about at home and at work will benefit from your journey through Up, Down, or Sideways."

DR. JOSEPH MICHELLI, *bestselling author of* The Zappos Experience

"Look for a better wave. . . . Mark's book is filled with fresh and useful advice on reinvention and new ways to thrive."

SETH GODIN, *author of* Poke the Box

"No matter what state you're in—Up, Down, or Sideways—Mark Sanborn brings you back to the core principles that never change, no matter where you are. If you want to act on a 'good should,' then you *should* read this book."

DR. MARSHALL GOLDSMITH, *million-selling author of the* New York Times *bestsellers* Mojo *and* What Got You Here Won't Get You There

"Mark is an extraordinary speaker and an outstanding leader who speaks with conviction and experience on success. The practical advice and pearls of wisdom throughout this book are worth studying, contemplating, and dissecting. Learn how to apply them in your business and in your life to create sustainable growth and prosperity in all you do."

DR. NIDO QUBEIN, *chairman of Great Harvest Bread Company and president of High Point University*

"Mark Sanborn continues to amaze with his relevant, why-didn't-I-think-of-that lessons for success in work and life. His latest great book, *Up, Down, or Sideways*, will help you keep all life's ups and downs in perspective—and you'll love his concept of Sideways. Who needs to read this book right now? Everybody does!"

KEN BLANCHARD, *coauthor of* The One Minute Manager *and* Lead with LUV

"No matter where you are in life—Up, Down, or Sideways—there's no question that reading and following Mark Sanborn's advice will have a dramatic impact on your greater personal and professional success. I read a lot of books, and I enthusiastically recommend that you read this one."

DARREN HARDY, *publisher of* SUCCESS *magazine and bestselling author of* The Compound Effect

"Mark Sanborn is refreshingly commonsensical and characteristically right on the money with *Up, Down, or Sideways*. Every book he's written has influenced my thinking, but this one has inspired my *doing*. Each chapter prompted me to act differently, think differently, and see differently. Regardless of whether you are Up, Down, or Sideways, these timeless principles will propel you forward."

DR. WAYNE CORDEIRO, *pastor of New Hope Christian Fellowship, Oahu, and bestselling author of* The Divine Mentor

Up, Down,

 Tyndale House Publishers, Inc., Carol Stream, Illinois

How to succeed when times are
good, bad, or in between

or Sideways

MARK
SANBORN

Library of Congress Cataloging-in-Publication Data

Sanborn, Mark.
  Up, down, or sideways : how to succeed when times are good, bad, or in between / Mark Sanborn.
     p. cm.
  ISBN 978-1-4143-6221-2 (hc)
  1. Success—Religious aspects—Christianity. I. Title.
  BV4598.3.S263 2011
  650.1—dc23   2011032759

Printed in the United States of America

17 16 15 14 13 12 11
7   6   5   4   3   2   1

To my father, Leslie Sanborn, who taught by example.

And to my sons, Hunter and Jackson.

I aspire always to do the same.

CONTENTS

THE GOOD SHOULDS

THE CANADIAN PUNK band Simple Plan released a song a few years back titled "Shut Up!" The lyrics include "Don't tell me what I should do / I don't wanna waste my time," and the chorus begins with "So shut up, shut up, shut up / Don't wanna hear it."

Not exactly a feel-good song for the ages, is it?

Unfortunately, it's easy to take that attitude when other people give us advice, even if most mature adults would never express the sentiment so bluntly. There are times when we all resist the advice that others offer us because it can feel controlling, and after all, we want to make our own decisions. We don't like other people telling us what we should do.

In resisting the "shoulds" in life, however, we often throw the baby out with the bathwater. While some advice can be critical or controlling, other advice is helpful and needed. I call the latter the "good shoulds."

My mother, and I suspect yours as well, would say things to me like "You should brush your teeth." "You should look both ways before you cross the street." "You should be kind to others." As we grow older, our parents, teachers, coaches, employers, pastors, friends, and mentors bring increasingly complex and specific advice to our burning ears.

Fortunately, informed and concerned people in our lives still give us things we *should* do—things that have stood the test of time and have proven to be true and valuable. Just because we're adults doesn't mean we learn only from our experiences and not from the mistakes and successes of others. Why learn only from your own blunders if you can take a cue from someone else's and avoid a few missteps? Why not learn from the lessons and experiences of others?

This book is unapologetically a discussion about things

you should do—indeed, things all of us should do. I read books for insights, and I write books to share good ideas that I believe will help others. But these "shoulds" are borne of concern and my own life lessons and missteps, not out of a desire to control or manipulate. It's up to you to decide what to do with them.

Our doctors, accountants, attorneys, spouses, friends, coworkers, pastors, investment counselors—they all weigh in on what we should do. And when we have good advice available to us, we should take it. Wise people seek out and act on "good shoulds."

The mind-sets and methods in this book are based on principles, and principles don't change. They are true across time, culture, and context. What changes is the application. The principles of communication, for instance, haven't changed throughout history. Communication happens when you express a message in a way that people know and understand what you mean and can act on it. The applications—from longhand letters to faxes to e-mail to Facebook—have changed dramatically as cultures and technologies have advanced. But the core principles of communication haven't changed.

The core principles that drive success haven't changed either. Some of the applications have shifted, but the principles remain the same. They are good advice. You should use them, and so should I. And we should all share them with others. (With all due respect to the band Simple Plan.)

—*Mark Sanborn*

SECTION 1: SEE

It sounds simple, doesn't it? From infancy we are able to see the world around us. But seeing isn't just about looking at the world around you; it's about attaching meaning to what you see. One person might see a daunting wave; a surfer sees an opportunity. One person might see an obstacle; a successful person sees a starting block. Are you willing to open your eyes?

"The value of experience is not in seeing much, but in seeing wisely."

—WILLIAM OSLER, CANADIAN PHYSICIAN

CHAPTER 1

THE SURFER'S SITUATION

Interact with the waves of change to create the outcome you desire.

THE TRIPLE WHAMMY hit me three years ago. For one thing, speaking engagements—my primary source of income—had dropped by about 20 percent. For another, my financial investments tanked. And last but certainly not least in the Sanborn Triad of Trials, doctors diagnosed me with prostate cancer.

Strike one. Strike two. Strike three. Right?

Well, not quite. It certainly wasn't a home-run year, but then again, I know people who have faced much worse.

Besides, it was only half an inning in the long game of life. And to my surprise, that year of setbacks ended up leading me to a huge positive: fresh insights.

Like most insights, mine had been developing in the crucible of time—not just days, but months or even years before. I have no idea how long they had been percolating in my heart and mind. But I do know they came together with great clarity while I lay in bed for eight days that December convalescing from prostate surgery.

I wouldn't know until the end of those eight days that the surgery had stopped the spread of the cancer, so contemplative thoughts about life's uncertainties filled my downtime. I read books, newspapers, and magazines until my vision blurred, and then I turned to the television. The programming, like the reading material, greeted me with reports of the global economic meltdown and worsening recession—as if I needed reminders that my business and investments were down.

Faith, family, and friends aren't the desserts that follow the big meal of success; these are success.

Things were tough globally, too. It didn't seem to matter

much where you lived on the planet—everyone was affected by the financial crisis.

I pulled out of the stock market just about the time it hit the bottom and started back up. Many experts, including the really smart one who advised me at the time, felt the market would retest the bottom, providing a soon-to-come perfect opportunity to get back in. It didn't.

My business portfolio wasn't doing much better. As an author and professional speaker, I earn a large part of my income from speaking at meetings. Several high-profile corporations were getting hammered in the media (and even by Congress) for excessive spending on their events, so the meetings industry—that is, the opportunity to practice my livelihood—was nearly as depressed as the stock market.

I've had downturns in business. I've had downturns in finances. And I've had downturns in health. But until that year, I had never felt the distress of all three at the same time.

As odd as it might sound, however, nothing going on at that time—nothing I was reading or watching, nothing that had happened in my personal life, and nothing the doctors might tell me in the forthcoming days—could shake my feeling that I was still blessed.

Why?

Well, for starters, as simple as it sounds, I was overwhelmed by reminders of the importance of faith, family, and friends. These aren't the desserts that follow the big meal of success; these *are* success, at least as I have come to define it.

I don't know of a universally shared definition of success, but I do know it's always about more than material wealth. I've had the opportunity to develop a diverse range of friendships—from salt-of-the-earth people of simple means to millionaires and billionaires. I can count on one hand those who define success singularly or even primarily as "net worth." When pressed for more than a superficial answer, most people I've asked define success as the quality of their lives. That includes things like health, meaningful work, relationships, service, leisure, learning, and faith. These things all blend together to create that thing we call success.

The other reason I still felt a sense of prosperity was that I knew my challenges, as tough as they seemed, were met head-on by strategies I'd practiced throughout my adult life. In other words, while my lot in life wasn't as good as it had been, there were several identifiable reasons why it wasn't as bad as it could have been. I realized that almost everything knocking me down at the time came from forces outside my control, but there were several things I had been doing for years that mitigated the negative effects.

My bookings for meetings were down, but not nearly as much as they were for other speakers—I knew of some whose bookings were off 70 percent. I believe years of hard work developing a reputation for delivering value (in every sense of the word) provided the sure footing that kept me from sliding any further backward.

If you want to succeed when times are Up, Down, or Sideways, you have to learn how to identify and interact with forces bigger than yourself.

And while my investments had taken a significant hit, I was nowhere near the poorhouse. I grew up on a farm in Ohio, and my father's frugality bordered on obsessive. His father had lived through the Great Depression, and my dad drilled into me the most important and perhaps least complex financial planning tool there is: spend less than you make. So while I'd seen a dramatic drop in the value of my investments, I still had reserves.

Lying in bed in the days following my surgery, my physical prognosis still hung in the balance. But I knew I had done several things to speed my recovery. As an overweight kid who didn't like getting picked on, I had turned to exercise. I had worked out my entire adult life, and while I never reached competitive levels in athletics, I did develop an active lifestyle. I'm sure that aided my recovery. Eight days after my surgery, I was back on my exercise bike (with my surgeon's blessing).

No matter who you are, at some point circumstances will come that are outside your control. But there are things you can do to help you succeed even in challenging times. These, in fact, are the things you and I should do whether times are Up, Down, or Sideways. And that's what this book is about: how to maximize the upsides, mitigate the downsides, and succeed as much as you can all the time.

CATCHING THE WAVE

In business, we're told to be proactive. But let's be clear: proactivity has its limits. Proactivity is about what we choose to do but not always about what we control. And much of what we deal with in life falls outside of our control.

To prove it, pick up a copy of the *Wall Street Journal* or your local newspaper and count the number of articles you controlled or influenced. Every day the count is the same for me: zero. Even if you are mentioned in the newspaper, you probably had little control over the article. The best you might hope for is that they spelled your name correctly. So while you can be proactive on a personal level about doing things, there are forces bigger than you that you cannot control or influence.

On the other hand, we also know that being reactive in business is the kiss of death. If you spend your life reacting to what happens, you'll end up, as my mother warned me, a day late and a dollar short.

So we find ourselves in a psychological dilemma: if

being reactive is the kiss of death and being proactive beyond a personal level is a myth, what's left?

The answer: *be interactive.*

Think of a surfer. Only the Creator can make and control a wave. But a good surfer finds and interacts with the waves to create the outcome he or she desires. Don't miss that first part: good surfers *look for good waves.* They are proactive on a personal level. They don't just say, "There's the ocean—let's surf!" They watch the weather, scout the shoreline, check with friends, and do whatever they can to find the best waves.

If you want to succeed when times are Up, Down, or Sideways, you have to learn how to identify and interact with forces bigger than yourself—the economy, your upbringing, government regulations, natural disasters, and on and on the waves roll.

We don't control those forces any more than surfers control the waves. I didn't trigger the mortgage meltdown. I didn't cause corporations to back off on the number of speakers they hired. I didn't do anything to get cancer. Yet I was impacted by all those things and challenged by how I would respond to them. My opportunities for success depended in part on how well I interacted with them to create the outcomes I desired—just as great surfers do when they look for the best waves.

Again, there are no guarantees. No matter how good you are, sometimes a big wave slams you under the soup. Even the best surfers wipe out. Other times, no matter how much you want to surf, the waves aren't big enough. You can either paddle around or find something else to do.

Growing up north of Youngstown, Ohio, I remember listening to some guys in their twenties who had been laid off from the local steel mill. Television reporters asked them, "What are you going to do?" The typical answer went something like this: "My daddy was a steelworker, and my granddaddy was a steelworker. There's nothing else I can do." I remember, even at my young age, thinking, *Are you kidding me?*

My father was a farmer, and my grandfather was a farmer. Did that mean all I could be was a farmer? Of course not. In fact, the family farm wasn't something that interested my brother or me, so it was easy enough for us to chase our own dreams. But too many people spend their lives floating around in ankle-buster waves. When things are Sideways—when you aren't riding the big wave or getting slammed—maybe you need to go to the shore and seek another activity. You still can create desired outcomes, even if it's not from riding big waves.

That's the Surfer's Situation. If the waves are moderate and commensurate with your skills, you'll do fine. If they are too big, they will wipe you out. If they are too small, you won't be able to ride them. Like a surfer, you have to figure out how to interact with forces bigger than yourself to create the outcomes you desire—the outcomes you define as success. I believe this book can help you do that.

THE YOU ECONOMY

So, where are you as you read this book?

I don't mean physically, as in "I'm sitting on a plane" or "I'm outside on my deck." I mean, where are you in life?

Up? Down? Sideways?

Are things great? Did you just get the new job, the big raise, the big bonus, the marriage to the love of your life? Are you in the best shape of your life—physically, emotionally, financially, and spiritually? Are your children all

Eagle Scouts and National Merit Scholars who never get in trouble?

Or are things a mess? Did you just lose your job, discover someone close to you is dying, or find out your spouse left you for someone else? Are your children battling addictions, hanging out with the wrong crowd, and pushing you to your emotional limits? Are you shackled by debt?

Or is your situation in between? Maybe you're doing okay as you progress through life, having little expectation for anything better and no real threat. Do you feel, as Pink Floyd sang, "comfortably numb"?

I can't predict what will happen with the economy, and even if I could, it wouldn't tell me where you are now. We tend to think the economy affects everyone equally, but it doesn't. The economy might be screaming Up like never before, and you still might be unemployed or struggling to make ends meet. The economy might be Down or Sideways, yet you might be doing quite well.

As an economist by training, I have learned that most people are far more interested in their personal economy—the "You Economy"—than the economy at large. The economy is impersonal. *Your* economy is personal. As the saying goes, a recession is when your neighbor loses his or her job; a depression is when *you* lose your job.

The thing about the You Economy is that it comes with no guarantees. You can do everything right, and something may still go wrong. You can do some things wrong and survive anyway—perhaps even come out ahead. Great parents sometimes end up with rotten kids. High-achieving adults sometimes rise out of rotten homes.

There are no guarantees. But some things are predictable. They don't guarantee success, but they do increase the odds. They are a form of insurance because they provide the best path toward success in life.

You can plot this reality on a graph and see a bell curve. On the one end, you have dumb luck—those times when you do the wrong thing and it still works out. On the other end, you have informed misfortune—those times when you do everything correctly and things still fail. Those come out as relatively flat lines. They happen often enough to make the grid, but not enough to raise it significantly. In the middle, however, is sustainable success. These are the results you get by doing the things that work—the methods and mind-sets addressed in these pages.

You and I can't explain away informed misfortune. It's a mysterious reality, but a reality nonetheless. And we can't explain dumb luck. Denying its existence won't make it less real. But those two realities don't have to shape your approach to life. You can (and should) focus on the things you have some control over—the things that mitigate the downsides, increase the upsides, and allow you to succeed.

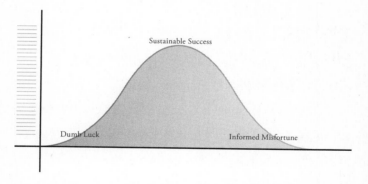

THE PRESENTOLOGIST

The late Sir John Marks Templeton was only a few years out of college when war began in Europe in 1939. The young investor from the back hills of Tennessee used borrowed money to buy one hundred shares each of 104 companies that were selling for one dollar per share or less. Thirty-four of those companies were bankrupt. But only four ended up worthless, and the shrewd but risky move launched Templeton's career. Some economic historians now consider him "the Father of the Mutual Fund."

Of course, he might have bet wrong. When it comes to picking stocks or predicting the course of the economy, the experts don't have a great track record. It has been joked that economists predict nine out of every four recessions. And it's not hard to find stories about animals that randomly pick stocks that outperform those selected by the best and the brightest financial analysts.

In *Future Babble: Why Expert Predictions Are Next to Worthless, and You Can Do Better*, Dan Gardner takes a look at an exhaustive research study done in the 1980s by Philip Tetlock. The research, he writes, shows that "experts' predictions were no more accurate than random guesses."

The point is, predicting the future is easy, but predicting it correctly is very hard. I can predict where the economy is going, but I can't know if I'm correct until we get there.

That's why I recommend against chasing success as a futurist. Instead, approach it as a "presentologist."

Rather than focusing on what might happen, focus on what you can do now to ensure you'll be successful regardless of what happens. Rather than trying to predict the future, prepare for it. Rather than anticipating what the world will *throw your way*, adopt and live out the timeless principles that will serve you, *come what may*.

There are things you can do some of the time to aid your efforts for success. And there are things you should do most of the time. And then there are a few things you should do all the time, regardless of circumstances. These are things that set you on a course toward sustainable success—whether times are Up, Down, or Sideways.

CHAPTER 2

BARRIER BASHING

We don't lack for knowing; we lack for doing.

NOT LONG AFTER his dad died, H. Jackson Brown Jr. was going through a closet and found eight shoe boxes filled with scraps of paper. It was his dad's collection of witty sayings about life, covering topics like self-reliance, commitment, love, and success.

Inspired, Brown turned them into *A Father's Book of Wisdom*, the first in a series of around twenty gift books that offer little more than one- or two-line inspirational quotes—some from Brown, some from his father, some from his mother, some from famous people, and some from unknown sources.

His third book, *Life's Little Instruction Book*, spent more than two years on the *New York Times* Best Sellers List. It includes more than five hundred sayings that he pulled together as a present for his son, Adam, as Adam left for college.

"Most of us know what we need to do to make our lives more fulfilled and useful," Brown once said, "but sometimes we forget. My little books are gentle reminders of those simple things which, if done well and in a spirit of love, can significantly change our lives."

This book comes with a similar offering, albeit in a different style and structure and with a somewhat different purpose. My goal isn't just to engage you and entertain you, although I wouldn't mind if that happened. I also want to educate and enrich you—to go a little deeper into the principles and then give you ideas you can use to succeed whether you are Up, Down, or Sideways. Famous quotes and clever sayings are great, but they don't really help us unless we put them into action.

If you're like me, you probably have far more great ideas

than you ever use in any given day. If I consistently did all the things I know I should be doing—all the things in Brown's books or even in the books I've written—I'd probably be retired on a yacht right now, sipping a cold beverage and enjoying tropical breezes.

I've come to believe that the greatest challenge we face as human beings is acting on what we know.

We don't lack for information nearly as often as we lack for application.

We don't lack for *knowing*; we lack for *doing*.

So here's that key question: what keeps us from doing what we know needs to be done?

The answer: barriers.

Barriers are obstacles and impediments that keep us from consistently acting on what we know.

In life, things simply get in our way and prevent us from doing what we want and need to do.

This book is about identifying and living out the methods and mind-sets that increase your odds for gaining and maintaining success, regardless of your circumstances. But you have to overcome some barriers to get there. You have to move beyond information and inspiration to action.

Before we get into strategies for overcoming common barriers, it will help to discuss the seven stages you might find yourself in whenever you face a call to action. Understanding them—and assessing the level you are at in the crucial areas of your life—is the first step toward bashing your barriers and moving where you know you need and want to go.

1. You don't know.

Ignorant is a negatively tinged word, but it simply means to lack knowledge. As the cliché goes, "You don't know what you don't know." It is so commonsensical that you can't argue the point, can you?

Even the best and brightest students don't learn everything in school or from their parents, from books, from mentors, or from playing video games (okay, I threw that last one in just for my kids). As adults, it is our

We don't lack for information nearly as often as we lack for application.

responsibility to discover the areas where we need to keep learning and growing, whether it's our work, our finances, or our spiritual disciplines.

MARK SANBORN || 23

Not only that, but sometimes we get bad advice. Sometimes we learn the wrong things, which keeps us from knowing and living out the right things.

Part of life is discovering options and becoming aware of what we need to know. So we keep reading, we keep asking questions, and we keep digging for undiscovered gold.

2. You know but don't believe.

Maybe you just need fresh insights on existing truth. You've heard something, but you don't believe it or you don't think it applies to your situation. You might even accept it at the head level, but not the heart level. You don't buy in. You don't internalize it. So you miss it.

Samuel Johnson, the eighteenth-century British author, put it this way: "People need to be reminded more often than they need to be instructed." That's why books like Brown's (and this one) serve a purpose even when they state what might seem obvious or when they state something that you, at first glance, don't think applies to your situation.

Perhaps you are Up or Sideways and you see no need to consider advice about what to do if you are Down. You may not think you need a cushion of savings or a healthy, active lifestyle . . . until the day you get slammed by an unexpected wave. Or maybe you are so deep in debt or out of shape that you can't imagine listening to any advice that seems directed at those who are experiencing good times. So you tune it out and don't take the information seriously.

3. *You know and believe but don't do.*

Very often we know and believe what we should do, but we simply don't do it. In other words, we lack conviction. Beliefs are things you hold; convictions are things that hold you. You can tell me who is important in your life (your stated belief), but your schedule shows your convictions. The same holds true with what you value and where you spend your money.

We usually know and believe but don't do for one of three reasons: it seems inconvenient, unnecessary, or difficult.

Consider this conversation between a son and his father:

"Son, I told you to put the dishes away."

"I know, Dad. I know."

"I know you know. But you aren't doing it. I've told you three times to put the dishes away!"

The dishes aren't put away because putting them away creates an inconvenience to a child who has something better to do. And what child can't find something better to do than putting dishes away?

Living out a principle we know and believe also might hit an obstacle if we see it as unnecessary. You might believe in putting money into your 401(k), and you might even have the funds to do it. But if times are good, you might not see the need. So you rationalize that your investments are doing just fine, and you spend the money on something else.

The third reason we know and believe but don't do is that doing something that's good for us isn't always easy. In fact, it's often difficult.

Beliefs are things you hold; convictions are things that hold you.

G. K. Chesterton, the prolific English writer, once pointed out that "the Christian ideal has not been tried and found wanting. It has been found difficult; and left untried." That's not just true of Christianity; it's true of most principles that are valuable. It's not that they don't work but that they're hard. So people stop trying them . . . or never try them at all.

4. You know and believe but can't do.

We often lack the skills and training to do the things that increase our odds for success whether we are Up, Down, or Sideways. When we face this obstacle, we can learn the skill or find someone who has the skills we lack to help us. For example, if you want to become proficient in a language, you could enroll in a course, get a DVD program, or find a tutor.

This book offers some skills and actionable ideas—specific things you can do to live out the principles. On other complex matters—high finance or physical or mental health, for instance—you might need to consult an expert in that field.

5. You know and do inconsistently.

H. Jackson Brown Jr., whose story is related at the beginning of this chapter, says this about our priorities: "Don't say you don't have enough time. You have exactly the same number of hours per day that were given to Helen Keller,

Pasteur, Michelangelo, Mother Teresa, Leonardo da Vinci, Thomas Jefferson, and Albert Einstein."

Unfortunately, we too often lack commitment or get distracted from doing the things that are important, and they never become part of our daily routines. What is keeping you from being consistent? Do you procrastinate, rationalize, or waste time online? Determine what's stopping you, and commit to making a change.

6. You know and do consistently.

Finally, you're getting something done! At this stage you know what to do, and you're doing it. You're going to the gym on a regular basis. You're eating dinner together as a family. You're putting a set amount aside for savings. Of course, you don't remain here consistently in every area. That's just life. You can't have it all, but you can work on the things that really matter.

Getting to this stage requires knowledge, understanding, commitment, hard work, and discipline—all areas I'll address throughout this book. It's my hope that by the final chapter you'll be prepared to work toward this stage and maintain it more consistently, regardless of whether you are Up, Down, or Sideways.

7. *You know and make it second nature.*

Consistency, while important to success, isn't the end of the line. When you know something and believe in it and do it consistently over time, eventually you reach a point where living out the principle becomes as natural as breathing. You don't have to think about whether to correct the cashier who just gave you too much change; you do it automatically because honesty is part of who you are.

At this stage, what you know is right takes a higher priority than what you feel. Our culture puts a great deal of emphasis on doing what feels right or what feels good rather than what actually is right and good. There are days when I don't feel like working out but very few days when I don't, at a deeper level, still want to do it. Exercise is part of my lifestyle. The same can be true in every area of our lives—with enough discipline, the right thing will eventually become second nature.

SEE THE CHALLENGES; APPLY THE SOLUTIONS

I titled the first section of this book "See" because I wanted to cover some foundational things you need to see—the challenges and realities you need to understand whether you are Up, Down, or Sideways. But as you now understand, awareness isn't always enough. How you think about what you see and know—the way you define success, your attitude, and your commitment to improving your thought processes—factors into what you'll eventually do with what you know.

In other words, ideas only benefit you when they are used. Will you simply collect old quotes, sayings, and insights, or will you make the effort to consistently apply these principles in your life? Let's start putting powerful ideas to good use.

SECTION 2: THINK

Thinking is easy, right? We do it all the time. Much of that thinking, however, is reactive. Few people take the time to intentionally develop the mind-sets that will help them deal with challenges and take advantage of opportunities. Mind-sets—the way we think— inform our methods, the things we do. Think about your thinking.

"Thought is action in rehearsal."

—AUTHOR UNKNOWN

CHAPTER 3

THE SCOREKEEPER'S SYSTEM

Change your scoring system;
change your game.

THE 2004 MOVIE *Alfie* tells the story of a charismatic limo driver who unapologetically spends most of his time pursuing relationships with as many women as possible.

In one scene, Alfie (played by Jude Law) says, "I myself subscribe more to the European philosophy of life, my priorities leaning towards wine, women. . . . Well, actually, that's about it."

Alfie, of course, never finds happiness by seeking

only the self-absorbed pleasures of life, and he eventually experiences heartbreak of his own. The film ends with Law's character delivering a monologue on his lifestyle. He has money, nice clothes, and a fancy car to drive. He's unattached and depends on no one. His life is his own. But, he acknowledges, he doesn't have peace of mind. And that haunts him.

"If you don't have that," he says, "you've got nothing. So . . . what's the answer? That's what I keep asking myself. What's it all about? You know what I mean?"

We don't know if Alfie finds an answer to that age-old question: what's it all about? We do know that each of us answers that question every day with the way we go about living life. As Ralph Waldo Emerson put it, "The ancestor of every action is a thought."

So how are your actions defining success? If you want to put yourself in a position to thrive regardless of whether times are Up, Down, or Sideways, then you have to understand how you define success.

I have posed the question "How do you define success?" to many friends and clients over the years. My primary conclusion? Success is specific to the individual. While there are some generalities that we apply to success, at the end of the day it is an individual definition.

I define success as living a life of learning, love, faith, and service. Those are my highest priorities. And while there are many other things I value and appreciate, they are secondary to these four objectives.

What's your definition of success? You have one, even if you've never thought about it or stated it. It is your personal answer to the Alfie question: what's it all about? In other words, what's important to you? How are you living it out?

Often we let others define our success. Parents, peers, teachers, counselors, the community, and the culture at large all offer suggestions, but ultimately we either choose our definition or live by a definition that is imposed on us. Some of the unhappiest people I know are those who have never come to terms with the question of what success is to them.

Unfortunately, many of us have a theoretical or philosophical definition of success (what we'd like it to be) and a very different functional definition (how we're living). Alfie's definition might have been something like, "To be happy and enjoy all that life has to offer," and yet he was miserable.

You can assess your definition of success (and your success at attaining it) by filtering your actions through the scoring system you use for your life. But here's the thing many people never realize: you have the freedom to choose your scoring system. And you can change your scoring system and change your game.

They are stuck using a scoring system that doesn't fit the game they really want to play.

THE FOUR R'S OF SCOREKEEPING

Henry James, the nineteenth-century writer, once said, "It's time to start living the life you've imagined." The problem is, most people have never imagined a life that's any different from the one they're living.

Why? They are stuck using a scoring system that doesn't fit the game they really want to play.

I've heard people in professions that traditionally don't pay much complain about how hard it is to make a living doing the thing they love. And I've heard financially wealthy people complain about how they never get to spend time with their kids because they have to work such long hours.

They all have an option: change their scoring systems. Unlike in sports, you don't have to play under someone else's rules. As long as it isn't illegal, immoral, unethical, or downright narcissistic, there are all sorts of systems available for scoring your version of success.

Most people organize their lives and their work around one of four scoring systems: results, recognition, recreation, or relationships. Those are not the only organizing systems, but they are the most common. There's overlap—we don't live by just one alone—but one of the four almost always sets the pace and influences the others, especially when there's a choice to be made between one priority and another. Your actions, not your intentions, tell you which priorities rule in your life.

If you organize around **results,** then you're all about achievements. You want to win the prize. You want to earn a certain income, drive a certain car, and live in a certain neighborhood. Those are your goals, and achieving your goals is what matters most.

Results are important, of course, and not all results are egotistical or self-focused. Your goal might be to give away one million dollars before you die. And most of us work in results-based careers—striving to achieve sales quotas, meeting deadlines, accomplishing the assigned tasks. But if achieving those results is the ultimate source of satisfaction in your life and not just a contributing factor, then that is your organizing system for scoring your life.

If you organize around **recognition**, then it's not enough to achieve things if those achievements are not noticed and acknowledged by others. You want to be known for making contributions. You are the actress who loves the stage over film because you long to hear the applause of a live audience. Or you want to win "Salesman of the Year" more for the prestige than for the bonus that comes with it. Or you volunteer mainly so people will tell you what a good person you are. You produce outstanding results by thriving on a steady diet of ego biscuits.

The third way to organize your life is around **recreation**. For you, work is a means to an end. You earn money not for recognition or accomplishment but because money lets you take vacations, play golf, ride jet skis, sail boats, and enjoy time with friends until the wee hours of the night. It's about living large and having fun. That's your scoring system—how much can you fish, hunt, ski, sail, hike, bike, dance, party, and play between those hours when you're forced to earn a paycheck.

The fourth organizing system is **relationships**. John Maxwell has said that success is when the people who know you the best respect you the most. I love that line because it speaks to both the quality of our relationships and our integrity. If relationships are your priority, people come first in your considerations and your motivations. You think *who* before *what*.

All the scoring systems shape your priorities and your definition of success, and all can shape them in positive ways. But for me relationships belong at the top of the priority list. Everything that happens because of us or to us happens in community. Victories are sweeter when shared, and difficulties are lessened with encouragement and support. There is no upside to going it alone. When I was recovering from my cancer surgery, it was clear to me that what mattered most were faith, family, and friends. And the heart of all three is relationships—my relationship with God, my relationships with my family, and my relationships with my friends.

No matter how efficient and effective and capable you are, there are things that are going to thwart your results and leave you empty-handed. No matter how much you do to earn the recognition and praise of others, there are some people you'll never please. Not everyone is going to give you the acknowledgment you deserve, much less what you desire. And you can have a house and a garage full of toys but no time to use them because you're too busy making money to buy them. Or you go into debt, leveraging your income and your time to buy and use things you really can't afford, a disease I once heard described as "affluenza."

But I've noticed that people who focus primarily on relationships tend to achieve more results because people cooperate with them and support them. They tend to get recognized for the right reasons because they really are concerned about how their actions affect others. Their recreation becomes an extension of their relationships, so they not only make the time to enjoy life but they also do so with the people who matter most to them. Their lives aren't solitary or shallow or self-focused. Even when people fail them—and we always fail each other because we're human—the higher calling of serving others still provides victories.

YOU CAN'T HAVE IT ALL

A pastor I know likes to say, "The bad news is you can't have it all. The good news is, when you know what's important, you don't want it all anyhow."

The unhappiest people are the ones trying to have it all. They want super-successful careers. They want to earn high incomes. They want manicured lawns. They want to exercise, eat right, and live large. They want respect and praise from others. They want to travel the world. And even though they spend two hundred days a year on the road, they want thriving marriages and great relationships with their kids. Mostly, they want more—more of what they already have and more things they see others with but don't yet have themselves.

Your actions, not your intentions, tell you which priorities rule in your life.

Reality check: you can't have it all. But that's all right. As those noted philosophers the Rolling Stones put it, "You can't always get what you want / But if you try sometimes, well you might find / You get what you need."

So as you go about defining success and your scoring system for measuring it, here are a few tidbits of advice that might help you figure out not just what you want but what you need.

CLARIFY YOUR SCOREKEEPING SYSTEM

Be clear about what's important to you. A lot of people are leaning their ladders against the wrong walls. They are working hard to achieve things that they really don't want. They have adopted someone else's vision of success, and they're using someone else's scoring system. Your trusted friends and advisers can help you figure out what's important to you, but they can't give you the answer. Frankly, it's your definition . . . and your responsibility.

Be clear about why it's important. Is it your priority because that's what your wife wants you to do? Because that's what your faith dictates? Because you've invested years into it? Because your mother always wanted it for you? You need clarity not just on the *what* but on the *why*, because it will either change your course or confirm it. Once again, this is a question you need to answer for yourself because only you know what's in your heart and your belief system. You have to own the *why*.

When I was a junior at Ohio State, I came upon a friend who was busy memorizing the body parts of a cat. He was a premed major. So I asked him why he wanted to be a doctor. "Because my dad and my grandfather were docs," he said. It made me wonder. Did he really want to become a doctor? Did he do it just because it was expected of him? Had he seriously considered other career choices?

The lesson I took away from my future doctor friend is this: you can enlarge your expectations by considering your options and what is most important to you. Before we decide what to become, it behooves us to consider all the possibilities.

Be honest about the cost. In economics, we talk about opportunity costs versus hard costs. A purchase, project, service, or venture may only cost you X out of pocket, but it may cost you ten times that in terms of what you could have earned if you had deployed those resources differently. I'm not saying that cost should be your driving factor in every decision; I'm saying you need to understand the costs because you'll have to live with them.

Your love for a particular profession or for doing volunteer work or for spending time with your children might mean you'll never earn a six-figure income. Or your desire to help your son attend the college of his dreams might mean you're willing to spend a few years working longer hours to pay for it. You might reject a new business opportunity because the other party wants a kickback or because you know the product, while rich in profit potential, doesn't line up with your morals.

The costs can be financial, relational, or ethical. But if you consider the cost on the front end, it's much easier to live with the bill each month or to decide not to make the purchase at all.

Be honest about the commitment. What's it going to take to achieve your definition of success, not just in terms of money but also in terms of time and energy?

Francis Chan is an example of someone who redefined success and changed the scoring system of his life. In 1994

Chan founded a church in Simi Valley, California, and saw it grow to one of the largest congregations in Ventura County. He wrote a couple of bestselling books and launched a college. But his heart (and his life's message) was about giving his life away to people in need. So in 2010 he stepped down from his church-leadership role to work directly with the urban poor. In other words, he committed his time and energy (and money) to achieve his definition of success.

NOW HIT THE STREET

Once you're clear on what's important to you and why, and once you've counted the costs and honestly considered the commitment, then the other stuff drops away. Living it out isn't so daunting. You're ready to go to work putting your priorities into action.

You might be ten pounds overweight, but you know that's not going to kill you and it's a price worth paying because you value your love of cooking. Or you might have to give up twenty-five thousand a year in commissions, but it's worth it because you won't miss your kids' plays. Or you might feel compelled to run for the school board, so you're willing to give up the time and privacy that come with holding a public office. You might want to join Francis Chan serving the urban poor, or you might want to devote your life to politics, science, economic theory, disaster relief, or energy innovation. There are worlds of possibilities for you to accomplish your goals, professional and otherwise.

If you really examine what's important to you and why, and if you count the costs and gain clarity on the commitment, I'm convinced you won't end up as a self-absorbed Alfie. You'll own your version of success, and you'll use your own scoring system to attain it. And in the process, you'll discover that success really is all about the life you lead, the impact you make, and the legacy you leave.

CHAPTER 4

THE OPTIMIST'S ORIENTATION

*The difference between obstacles and
opportunities is your outlook.*

BEFORE WE GET into this chapter, I should make a confession: I have a predisposition to see the negative, and on bad days I tend to "catastrophize." I'm not going to psychoanalyze why that is—genetics? environment?—but I take full responsibility. I don't like this about myself, and it doesn't serve me well. That's why I've become convinced of two things.

First, our modern understanding about the value of optimism is founded on legitimate research. The positive thinking that cynics tend to make fun of suddenly has newfound credibility in light of solid research.

Second, we can change our thinking despite our disposition. If you already have the Optimist's Orientation, that is terrific. This chapter will reinforce it and maybe provide some additional insights. If, like me, you tend to see the glass as half-empty, you can learn what you need to do to override negativity as a way of life.

THE VALUE OF OPTIMISM

My friend Don Hutson considers himself a "reverse paranoid"—he believes everyone is out to help him!

He sees the donut, not the hole.

Pick your cliché about optimists, and Don exemplifies it.

But here's the question: so what?

Don is successful in business and in life, but does optimism really have anything to do with his success? And, more personally, does optimism really matter to your success or mine?

T. O. White said, "Extreme optimists and extreme pessimists are usually wrong, but the former have more fun being that way."

The reality is, most of us appreciate optimism. Indeed, we start most endeavors unrealistically optimistic in light of the harsh truths of statistical probabilities. Study after study finds that most students start each semester believing they will make As in their courses, most newlyweds believe they'll never experience divorce, and most entrepreneurs believe their new ventures will succeed. Failure? That's for the other guys.

How well do most people live out that optimism in the long term? Rather poorly, it seems, especially when times get difficult. Reality often becomes the pin that deflates the balloon of hope. The student misses a few classes, falls behind on her reading, and suddenly aspires to a C rather than an A. The newlywed discovers all his spouse's annoying habits and the reality that even the best relationships require hard work. And the entrepreneur discovers unexpected staffing challenges and cash flow pitfalls.

If times are Up or Sideways, on the other hand, optimism can lose its place as a priority in day-to-day affairs. We can chuckle at jokes about optimists, and we can give a cursory nod to the power of positive thinking, but all too often we then strip it of its significance by pushing it into a corner with life's other clichés. We have work to do, after all.

Plus, we realize there's another side to what we typically think of as optimism: foolishness. It is seen in the silly denial of the guy who doesn't consider that the light at the end of the tunnel might be an oncoming train.

That's fair and valid, but surviving, much less prospering, when times are Up, Down, or Sideways simply won't happen without an Optimist's Orientation. As Helen Keller said, "Optimism is the faith that leads to achievement. Nothing can be done without hope and confidence."

FROM HELPLESSNESS TO HAPPINESS

Martin Seligman, often called "the Father of Positive Psychology," was on a team in the 1960s that discovered learned helplessness. When people don't believe they can change or escape a bad situation, they learn to accept it, so much so that they often assume things are out of their control even when they are not.

MARK SANBORN || 51

In one famous experiment, people were placed in three groups. One group heard an annoying noise but could turn it off with the push of a button. Another group heard the same noise but were unable to turn it off no matter what they tried. The third group heard no noise. The next day, all three groups were exposed to a new situation that involved an annoying noise, and this time all of them could turn it off with minimal effort. The people in the first and third groups simply turned off the noise, but those in the second group typically did nothing. That's what Seligman calls learned helplessness.

Optimism isn't just prescriptive medicine to prevent depression and anxiety. It's also a component of success.

But about one-third of people never become helpless, Seligman notes. They don't give in to the idea that yesterday's bad experience is a predictor of today's misery. Why?

Optimism.

"We discovered that people who don't give up have a habit of interpreting setbacks as temporary, local, and changeable," Seligman writes in the *Harvard Business Review*. "That suggested how we might immunize people against learned helplessness, . . . against giving up after failure: by teaching them to think like optimists."

But optimism isn't just prescriptive medicine to prevent depression and anxiety. It's also a component of success.

Shawn Achor spent ten-plus years at Harvard researching happiness, as well as analyzing the research of others on the topic. In his 2010 book *The Happiness Advantage*, Achor explains that more than a decade of groundbreaking research in positive psychology proves that happiness doesn't result from achievement and success (financial or otherwise); instead, achievement and success (financial or otherwise) result from happiness.

This proves true in pretty much every area of life— marriage, community involvement, friendship, health, and work.

"Data abounds showing that happy workers have higher levels of productivity, produce higher sales, perform better in leadership positions, and receive higher performance ratings and higher pay," Achor writes. "They also enjoy more job security and are less likely to take sick days, to quit, or to become burned out. Happy CEOs are more likely to lead teams of employees who are both happy and healthy, and who find their work climate conducive to high performance."

Optimism, in turn, is a key to happiness and success. "If you believe your behavior matters, we find that ultimately increases your success rates," Achor said in an interview recorded for Success.com.

Intelligence and technical skill factor into only 25 percent of a person's chances for success, he said. The other 75 percent is made up of your optimism, the support of your social network, and your attitude toward stress (whether you view it as a challenge or a threat). So your optimism, the optimism of those around you, and your attitude about stress (optimism under pressure) account for three-fourths of your success.

In other words, as Achor writes, "happiness and optimism actually *fuel* performance and achievement."

If you want success, if you want to achieve great things—not to mention fend off depression and anxiety—then you first need to run out and get you some optimism, right?

I'm buying—how about you? Just point me toward that store!

Of course, we can't buy optimism. Not only that, but we

can't create it through hard work. That's what makes it so elusive—we don't get it by what we do but by how we view the things we do. As Achor puts it, "The mental construction of our daily activities, more than the activity itself, defines our reality."

This is the Optimist's Orientation. The way you look at yourself and the world around you affects your success, regardless of the circumstances.

FRAMING YOUR OPTIMISM

The lens you use to view yourself and the world doesn't change reality, but it shapes your view of yourself and your situation and, thus, how you respond. Your attitude predisposes how you see the world and what you do about it.

Attitude isn't everything, but it is the first thing. Why try if you don't think you can succeed? At some level, you need to try with a belief that you really can accomplish your goal. Otherwise you are looking through a lens shaded by defeat.

So to properly frame your orientation for optimism, here are some ways you need to consider viewing yourself and the world.

Be skeptical but not cynical. Skeptics withhold judgment until they have more information. Cynics aren't looking for more information; they assume (and thus invite) the worst.

You need to be informed without becoming cynical. Optimists raise questions, seek answers, and pay attention to any information that might help them make wise decisions and prepare for the challenges of life. As former British prime minister Harold Wilson said, "I'm an optimist, but I'm an optimist who takes his raincoat."

Choose reality over fantasy. Whenever there is a downturn, some leaders and managers preach a mind-set of intentional naiveté.

This mind-set is best summed up in this headline from a blog: "I Refuse to Participate in a Recession." That, of course, is like saying you are going to stand in the middle of a snowstorm but choose not to get cold or wet. You can deny the storm, but that doesn't change the reality of the weather. More to the point, successful individuals and companies aren't refusing to participate in the economic downturn; rather, they are successful despite it.

Let's face it: denial is a poor strategy. You have to

acknowledge what's happening and then choose how you interact with the circumstances.

Think on the noble *and* the necessary. The Optimist's Orientation is about what you think on. There are those who believe an optimist should *only* think about things that are positive. For instance, I read a blog post encouraging people to stop reading the newspaper because it's full of negativity. This is denial through avoidance, and it makes for a poor strategy. You need to make informed decisions about things such as where to live, when to sell your home, the safety of a park you might stroll through at night, the politicians who want your vote, the schools where you might send your children, and the businesses you might frequent.

Attitude isn't everything, but it is the first thing.

If you only think on the positive and ignore the negative, you'll create a mismatch between your information and reality.

The Bible offers some great advice about where to focus your thoughts: "Whatever is true, whatever is noble, whatever is right, whatever is pure, whatever is lovely, whatever is admirable—if anything is excellent or praiseworthy—think about such things" (Philippians 4:8).

But notice that it doesn't say never to think about other things. It says there is more to be gained by focusing on the positive than by focusing on the negative. That's what the Optimist's Orientation is all about. It isn't about denial or choosing ignorance over information. It isn't about being uninformed or misinformed. It's about being *fully informed*, then choosing to focus on the good instead of the bad.

Elevate your view. You need to be informed, but it can't stop there. When you view yourself and the world, you must be informed *and* inspired to action. Information by itself doesn't move you.

How you view yourself and how you view the world goes a long way toward how informed you are, how inspired you become, and how you express that inspiration in your actions. And a full perspective allows for a clear view.

My office in Denver used to be due west of my home. It was funny how many days I'd drive to work and never notice the majestic Rocky Mountains. Every day they were right there in front of me, if only I'd remember to look up.

I had the choice to draw on that inspiration or miss it. I could look down and see dirt or pavement, or I could look up and see mountains and majesty.

Try a different perspective. *Scientific American Mind* once ran an article titled "Mind over Magic?" that explored how our habits of perceptions and brain functions are key to successful magic acts. A few months later, the magazine ran a letter from a reader who attested to that truth. It seems he was tired, so he lay on his side while watching a television special by a magician. His head was horizontal rather than vertical, and that little shift allowed him to see beyond the illusions.

"Somehow lying down did not provide the implicit body cues associated with all those learned expectations," he wrote, "so my attention was not led in the normal way."

I've never lain down to watch a magic show, but the letter writer was right—successful magic is all about your perspective. So is your Optimist's Orientation.

Perception isn't reality, but it shapes your reality. Changing your perspective doesn't change what is; it changes how you see what is. Reality doesn't change. The economy is going to be Up, Down, or Sideways regardless of whether you are lying down or sitting up. But your perspective affects how you interpret what you see. Looking at things differently and with a fresh perspective can help you see through the illusions of life and embrace slices of reality you didn't know existed.

Find the humor. I'm reminded of a story about an eternal optimist. He lived by the motto "You can choose to be in a good mood or a bad mood," and he always tried to choose the good mood. This approach was tested when he was critically injured in a fall from a communications tower. As he was wheeled into the emergency room, the expressions on the faces of the doctors and nurses all communicated the same message: *he's a dead man.*

Then one of the nurses asked him if he was allergic to anything.

"Yeah," he said. "Gravity."

As the laughter died down, he added, "I'm choosing to live. Operate on me as if I'm alive, not dead."

Humility and *humor* come from the same root word. We're humbled because we know how funny life can be. We're able to laugh at life because in our humility we realize we don't control everything. Humor isn't always apparent, especially in difficult situations. The optimist searches it out.

I mentioned that optimism is something I've needed to learn. The good news is, I've seen the funny in almost everything. The ability to find the humor in difficult situations has enabled me to keep my cool and sometimes my sanity. I love a good practical joke, whether I'm the prankster or the victim, because it reminds me not to take myself—or everything that happens in life—too seriously.

Focus on the victory, not the loss. In my work with corporate America, especially during the Down economy, the most common problem I see among managers is that they stop playing to win and start playing not to lose.

In times of recession we all know what we're afraid of and what we don't want to happen, but we often lose sight of what we are trying to make happen. But people don't gravitate toward negative goals.

Does this only happen during a recession? Not when you think of the You Economy. It doesn't matter what's going on in the world; you still might only play defensively. My grandfather, for instance, lived an extremely cautious life even in the best of economic times, largely because he remembered the bad times of the Great Depression.

You might be a cautious and conservative person, and I'm not saying that's bad. You can (and should) be prudent when playing to win. Playing not to lose isn't being prudent; it's focusing on the wrong things. Playing to win means understanding potential problems and obstacles, avoiding unnecessary risks, and at the same time pursuing opportunities for prosperity.

Playing to win requires both a good offense and a good defense. We all know the best athletic teams have both (and don't forget those special teams). It's not an either/or.

Perception isn't reality, but it shapes your reality.

When you face setbacks, FIDO! My buddy Clebe McClary lost an arm and an eye serving America in Vietnam, and his sacrifices earned him a Man of Valor award. Like many soldiers of that time, however, Clebe didn't always receive a warm reception after he came home. But his Optimist's Orientation helped him deal with adversity and setbacks by living out a principle known as

FIDO: Forget It; Drive On. Instead of rehearsing the difficulties of his past, he focused on what he learned and dedicated his life to inspiring others, both through his career as a speaker and through his work with inmates.

Clebe understands that life isn't perfect. There are setbacks, even for an optimist. So you control what you can, acknowledge what you can't, learn from mistakes and defeats, and keep moving forward. Don't ignore what has happened—that's a form of denial—just don't let what has happened slow you down. Extract the lesson and move on.

A ROOM WITH A VIEW

It was my first trip to Rome. I had finally made the time to visit one of the cities of my dreams, and I was excited. The cab let me out in front of the Hotel Eliseo, near the Via Veneto, and the reception desk manager told me I had a room on the first floor.

"Do you have a room with a view?" I asked.

He paused, deliberated purposefully, and let me know in no uncertain terms that he was doing me a great favor by giving me a room on the fifth floor. "A panoramic view!" he exclaimed.

The bellhop helped me get my bags to the room. I walked to the balcony and took in a breathtaking view of the city. It couldn't have been lovelier.

Suddenly I heard a noise I can liken only to a violent earthquake. It was coming from the wall behind the head-board of my bed—a great shaking and gnashing of steel. After a little investigation, I discovered it was the elevator equipment. Every time somebody pushed the elevator but-ton, I was treated to that monstrous rumbling.

Then it hit me: what a metaphor for life! The perfect view accompanied by the elevator shaft. The good and the bad, the beautiful and the ugly, side by side.

Some people try to deny the elevator shafts in life, but that's hard to do. And pretending they aren't there doesn't change anything. Others never notice the panoramic view. They can't get past the noise the elevator is making.

Neither denial nor negativity serves us well. Wisdom accepts the good and the bad but chooses to pay more attention to the good. Wise travelers in life don't dismiss the bad. If they can do something about it, they do. But if they can't, they don't bemoan what they can't change.

It isn't that we get the view *or* the rumbling; most of the time we get both. But you and I choose which one we focus on. We can dwell on the ugly or the beautiful.

CHAPTER 5

THE LEARNER'S LEVERAGE

If you aren't learning, you're losing out.

AUGUSTE RODIN ORIGINALLY called it *The Poet*—a bronze and marble sculpture of Dante. We know it better as *The Thinker*.

Rodin depicted Dante looking over the gates of hell while contemplating "Inferno," a major section in his epic poem *The Divine Comedy*. The first cast, created in 1902, is now in the Musée Rodin in Paris, but there are also around twenty additional "original" castings of the Frenchman's best-known work of art. They all depict a man looking thoughtful and somber, apparently experiencing a profound internal struggle.

Notably, *The Thinker*'s right elbow rests on his left knee.

You can't sit comfortably in that position. Try it.

So in addition to all the other meanings you might find in the sculpture, there's also this: thinking is not only important; it's also difficult. In fact, it can be downright painful at times. But it's necessary for success.

BUILDING BEHAVIORAL FLEXIBILITY

Making the most of your thinking provides critical leverage for dealing with the battles you face whether you are Up, Down, or Sideways. The more you learn, the more prepared you are for whatever comes your way. And the more you learn, the more you develop behavioral flexibility that provides a distinct advantage over your competition. Your life (and mine) operates within a variety of systems, many of them overlapping (your work, your family, your bowling league, etc.). And according to the rules of behavioral flexibility, more flexibility gives you more control within the system.

In other words, if we're playing chess and I know four moves and you know eight, then you have the upper hand. If we are in a sales situation and I know how to deal with six objections and you know how to deal with twenty, then you'll almost always beat me. You have more flexibility in your chess moves and in your sales strategies because you know things I don't know.

It's not enough to have access to information in order to apply it, however. We need to be able to assess whether the information can be trusted. This has always been true. Case in point: you can go back to magazines from the 1920s and 1930s and find advertisements for radioactive pendants that were billed as a health tonic. Wearing the pendants around your neck, the ads claimed, would improve your health. People apparently paid money to hang a radioactive piece of metal around their necks. They accessed information and applied it without assessing things like the dangers associated with radioactivity.

So there's always been a need for assessment. The difference today is in the volume of information we need to assess.

The difference is in the exabytes.

THE DATA DELUGE

A University of Southern California study released early in 2011 calculated that the world now has enough capacity in digital memory and analog devices to store more than 295 exabytes of information. That's 295 followed by twenty zeros, for those, like me, who don't often deal in exabytes.

The study also found that the world's computing capacity grew 58 percent a year from 1986 to 2007, the time range for the study.

It probably isn't news to you that human beings are creating, storing, sharing, and attempting to process more information than ever. We all feel the data coming at us from every direction, so much so that we don't always know what to do with it.

In fact, research now shows that our brains reach a point where the frustration, stress, and overload of too much information actually causes poor decision making. It has been dubbed "info-paralysis."

We typically do one of three things with information: we pay attention to it, we act on it, or we file it. Now we increasingly take a fourth option: we decide not to decide—we ignore the information. We look at all the information on going back to school, finding a new job, or determining how to refinance a home, and we simply give up and don't try. We decide we don't really need those extra classes. The current work situation is fine. We can do the refinancing another time.

At best, succumbing to information overload gets you the status quo. But more often than not it sends you backward, because the world isn't maintaining the status quo. It's moving forward. You have to keep learning because things keep changing. If you aren't learning, you're sure to lose out. And the more you know, the more you need to learn.

THE ASSESSMENT INVESTMENT

So how can we assess the validity of information that comes our way?

First, **look at the source** (who or where it's coming from).

Very few people or organizations are neutral when

they hand out information. That doesn't make them bad; it just makes them human. In some cases, their bias makes them untrustworthy; in other cases, it's just data itself that shapes your view of the information they are promoting. The worst financial advice I ever got was from one of the smartest financial experts I've ever met. Even the most credible people aren't perfect, so we need to carefully consider their biases and opinions and compare their advice with that of others we trust.

Second, **look at the evidence** (the validation from credible research and experts).

Much of the support for the information you find on the Internet focuses on anecdotal results. One website, for instance, claims that a well-known celebrity wears a "scalar energy pendant." This information is part of the site's "proof" that the pendants will, among other things, increase your energy and strength.

Not long after my cancer diagnosis, a friend suggested that I take a supplement, a rare metal once prescribed as a treatment for tuberculosis. The booklet she sent me was long on drawn-out anecdotes but short on any evidence proving the validity of the claims or efficacy of the supplement.

Contrary to popular belief, data is not the plural of anecdote. You can use anecdotes to support data, but the anecdotes themselves aren't valid data. In other words, the fact that three people took a particular supplement and got better doesn't tell me whether thousands of others took it and died.

Third, **look at the relevance** (the meaning for your situation).

Beware the habit of unexamined imitation. Just because a method worked for AT&T doesn't mean it works for the dry cleaner. Some strategies and tactics are transferable, and others aren't.

Or consider financial planning. Different information has differing relevance depending on a person's scoring system. How much risk you should take, in other words, depends on factors such as how old you are and what your goals are.

When you access information, assess its validity and relevance, and then apply the lessons learned from it, here's what you have: confidence.

Fourth, **look at yourself** (the personal "fit").

There are many things you can do, but ultimately you do what you believe is best given your hopes, fears, and preferences. Not all information—even valid information—is applicable to everyone. There are things I *can do* that I neither like to do nor need to do. There are times I could take on business commitments that would impinge on my ability to be a good husband or father. In those instances I pass on what I could do and go with what I need and want to do. To paraphrase Peter Drucker, I see no point in trying to become the richest man in the cemetery. Figure out what is a good fit for you.

The more you know, the more you need to learn.

LEARNING TO LEARN

When I started my career as a speaker, I was honored to work as a lead trainer of Tom Peters's In Search of Excellence seminar based on the book with the same title.

Many of the other trainers at that time were basically copying Tom's material, stories, and illustrations. If Tom told a story about Toyota, they told a story about Toyota. But I never wanted to just tell Tom's stories (although we were certainly approved to do so). I wanted to learn how Tom thought. So I tried to find stories and examples that Tom might use if he were starting from scratch.

I believe that the reason I was one of the highest-evaluated trainers at that time was because I told my stories in ways that brought the same value as Tom's stories but were uniquely my own. It wasn't enough to do what successful people did. I wanted to learn the thought process behind their actions. In other words, I didn't want them to tell me *what to think*; I wanted them to teach me *how to think*.

What I've learned over the years is that great thinkers—those who thrive in any circumstance—approach life with the following habits for thinking and learning.

Make investigation and inquiry a way of life. The son of a friend has a T-shirt that reads, "I gotta know," and it fits him perfectly. He is one of those kids whose favorite response to any answer is, "But why?" If you want to keep learning, keep asking the childlike questions, especially the *why* questions. Then dig out the details. Challenge yourself with the things you read, the places you go, the things you watch, and the people you get to know. Ask more questions. Ask better questions. Ask more people. Ask different people.

Ask. Ask. Ask.

Read. Read. Read.

Listen. Listen. Listen.

It seems so simple, yet so few of us do it.

Think for yourself. A lifestyle of investigation and inquiry provides tons of information and plenty of opinions, but none of those opinions are more important than your own. Think critically, even when—no, *especially* when—it is inconvenient. Remember to look at the source, look at the support, and look at the relevance. Then listen to your intuition, and draw your own conclusions.

Learn in the future tense. Living as a presentologist doesn't mean you shouldn't think about and prepare for the future. The more you learn, the more you know what you need to learn to adapt to a changing world around you. You can only become an expert on so much, and the best learners figure out where to spend their learning energy.

Watch the horizon: what technologies, topics, potential opportunities, or problems should you be exploring today to be prepared?

Design your own ongoing education program. As the old adage goes, plan your work and work your plan. You control your learning agenda—not only what you will study but the pace at which you'll study and the style of learning that works best for you. Your plan might include e-learning courses on leading great teams or in-person guitar lessons

Ask more questions. Ask better questions. Ask more people. Ask different people.

from a master teacher or books on rebuilding car engines or seminars on customer service. Regardless, the first step is to create the plan.

Make time to learn. Have you ever just "found" two hours to learn? Learning doesn't happen by accident, yet too many of us give too little time to the type of thinking that produces insights, allows us to internalize the lessons we've learned, and adds value to our lives and the lives of others.

Even in his mideighties, legendary speaker and author

Zig Ziglar says, "I still read three hours a day because I'm always thinking!"

We naturally tend to think reactively—we respond to questions, problems, and opportunities—but we don't make time to think proactively. So schedule time to read. Schedule time for seminars and training. And most important, schedule time to think. Think about what you've accomplished, what you've learned from recent successes and setbacks, how you are feeling, the relationships that need your attention, and what your vision is for the future (both personal and professional). I find it helpful to include prayer in this time as well. Seek insights into your thinking, into your learning. Seek wisdom to appropriately apply what you're learning.

Reflection usually requires getting away, which can mean physically relocating to a peaceful spot or simply closing your office door and turning off all of your interrupters (phones, computers, etc.). I know one guy who takes a sack lunch to a cemetery once or twice a week. No one bothers him there, and it probably reminds him not to waste the life he's living. Another guy puts a thirty-minute meeting with himself on his calendar every afternoon.

Leaders who value reflection make it a regular part of their schedules, and they benefit by turning their learning into leverage when times are Up, Down, or Sideways.

SECTION 3: DO

An often-quoted business maxim is that nothing happens until somebody sells something. The life corollary is that nothing happens until somebody does something. Mind-sets are important, but not enough. Doing the right things for the right reasons in the right way, and doing them consistently—that is what creates sustainable success.

"Take time to deliberate; but when the time for action arrives, stop thinking and go in."

—Napoléon Bonaparte

CHAPTER 6

PRODUCE VALUE

Value keeps you in the game.

A COLLEGE STUDENT named Kim needed a job, and because she had some experience working with video production, she decided to start her own little company. Using family connections, school connections, and social media, she put out the word that she was available to take VHS videos and convert them to digital formats.

Kim stayed busy, mostly taking home movies parents had made of their families and putting them into a format that would last longer and work with modern technology.

She knew from the start that her part-time job had a small window of opportunity before her customer base evaporated. But she seized the moment to use her skills solving a problem that people faced, and in doing so she made a little money to help pay her expenses.

Kim saw a need and provided value, which, of course, is the basis of all business. Value is the currency of commerce. If there were no need, her skills would lack value in the marketplace. And if there were a need and she lacked the skills, she would offer no value in the marketplace.

Value is the currency of commerce.

Individuals and organizations pay for what they value. And the organizations and individuals who get left behind in any economy are the ones that don't deliver what the marketplace values.

What's even more challenging is this: value is a moving target. I've seen the world go from vinyl records to eight-track tapes to cassettes to CDs to MP3s. And the value migration isn't over yet. There's always something new around the corner looking to render our newest must-have audio player obsolete.

Those who do the best in any economy are those who

know how to recognize and create value, whether as employees, employers, or entrepreneurs. In other words, succeeding when times are Up, Down, or Sideways ultimately depends on your ability to understand, create, and manage value.

And that's an active process. It requires that you act—that you do certain things. In short, you must create value, nurture relational value, make your value distinctive, protect your value, and appreciate value (all things we'll cover in the next few chapters).

If you want to mitigate the downsides and increase the upsides, you need to recognize that value is the currency that gets you a seat at the table. Extreme value—value that's nurtured, distinctive, protected, and appreciated—makes you a major player, regardless of the environment or circumstances.

VALUE PRODUCTION

No matter what happens in your work or your life, you ultimately need to create products, services, experiences, and ideas that people value.

Industries and companies that don't create value end up obsolete or, at best, get pushed into the corner as a niche market. But even those in a niche market must learn to create value—at least enough to survive within their self-defined scoring systems.

As individuals, our success at work—when times are Up, Down, or Sideways—hinges on our ability to consistently create value in the things we produce. We can do our jobs—prepare tax returns, operate the amusement park ride, work on the plumbing, ring up sales on a cash register, give speeches, sell insurance, or spend hours in the corner office with a C-suite title—and still create little or no value to others. The *process* isn't the *product*. What you *do* for a living isn't what people value; they value the *product* of your process.

Michael LeBoeuf, an author and retired management professor, once said the only two things people buy are solutions to problems and good feelings. For instance, several years ago I was at a resort swimming pool where a young lady was selling suntan oil. She told me all about the product—how it could solve my problems—and then she closed with this line: "If you'd like to buy this bottle of suntan oil for only $11.95, I'd be glad to apply it to your back for you."

Not only did I buy a bottle, but until I got married, I kept it in my medicine cabinet at home as a symbol of the only two things people buy: solutions to problems and good feelings.

So what's your product? And what's its value?

KEEPING YOUR PIPELINE FULL

To succeed when times are Up, Down, or Sideways, you have to produce things and experiences that people value, and you'd better have plenty of people who value what you produce. When others want what you are offering and are willing to pay you for it, it becomes proof that you are creating value. The key is to keep your pipeline full of the things people value and the people who value them.

Specifically, you need three inputs into your pipeline: important relationships, valuable projects, and potential customers. In Up times, all three are important; in Down times, they are critical.

Fill your pipeline with relationships. People are

important. Friends, family, coworkers, associates, people you've just met, people you interact with only briefly, your competitors, your customers. Well . . . everyone. People are important if for no other reason than that God has given us all intrinsic value. So creating value in your relationships—treating them as more than transactional—is important just because it's the right thing to do. And as a bonus, people factor into your chances for sustained success.

Creating relationships goes beyond mere networking to creating relationships in which you add value and gain value so that you have the support to succeed, to deal with success, and to mitigate troubles.

We'll look at nurturing these relationships in more detail in the next chapter, but it's important to start with the understanding that producing value in your relationships is foundational.

Fill your pipeline with projects. The politics of the federal budgeting process often bring the threat of a government shutdown. If that happens—as was the case in 1995—all "nonessential" federal workers go on furlough. They don't report to work (although they eventually get paid retroactively). The very thought of this sends the pundits screaming, "If they are nonessential, why do we have them on the public's payroll?"

Businesses that consistently operate with nonessential workers don't stay in business for long. Whether we're in management or not, we all need to add value to our organizations, and that starts with keeping our pipelines full of valued projects.

When times are Up, employers reward the people who are leading the most important projects. When times are Down, they lay off people who are working on the least important projects. If you create value in your projects, that gives you the best assurance that you won't get laid off in Down times. And when things are Sideways and raises become scarce, the best chance for getting one is if you have a mission-critical project.

Fill your pipeline with customers. You can never have too many customers—unless you have so many that you can't or don't take care of them all. But

Keep your pipeline full of the things people value and the people who value them.

that's a capacity issue. As the old sales adage goes, keep selling even when you have all the customers you need.

The only way to guarantee you'll always have all you need is to keep potential new customers in the pipeline.

The mortgage industry is a prime example. I've spoken in the mortgage industry for years, and in 2007 many home-owners who wanted to refinance their loans couldn't get a lender to return their calls. But when the industry hit the skids, the lenders were chasing refinance business hard because they needed customers with good credit ratings and they'd allowed their pipelines to go empty.

SURFING NEW WAVES

The *Yellow Pages* were once greatly valued by the American shopping public. The book arrived on America's doorsteps with easy-to-look-up listings of all sorts of businesses and services. Then it sat conveniently next to the telephone for easy access. Need a plumber? Look in the *Yellow Pages*. Need a new garage door? Look in the *Yellow Pages*. Need to pick a restaurant? Look in the *Yellow Pages*.

The printed version of the *Yellow Pages* still exists in most US markets, but technology has changed the emphasis and approach AT&T takes to that piece of its business. In the last few years, AT&T began reinventing the *Yellow Pages* as an online advertising company. The process is changing, but the promised result is the same: we can help you get more customers. That's AT&T's value proposition.

As you assess your own products—what is it that you produce that creates value?—it's important to live in the present and think toward the future. Your products and their value change over time, so you often have to change the product or the process. Sometimes it's a tweak. Sometimes it's an overhaul.

Most of us don't change until we have to. When it comes to value, we know what it has looked like in our past, we are less familiar with what it looks like in our present, and we are clueless about what it will look like in our

Success is an early warning indicator for failure.

future. All the while, we experience a slow degradation of our value. As author Seth Godin puts it, we typically do the things that work and keep doing them even after they stop working. Or as I often tell my corporate audiences, success is an early warning indicator for failure.

EVERLASTING VALUE

To make sure your production is valued and will be valued for the foreseeable future, you have to break out of that model. You don't do that by trying to predict and go after the next big jobs of the future. You do it by continuing to create value in an ever-changing environment.

Service, for instance, will always be valued, even if the ways we deliver service change. Excellence. Professionalism. Hard work. Dedication. Leadership. Ingenuity. Creativity. Perspective. All of these are "value adds" that you can take into any job or apply to any task. Why not develop them more fully?

Another value is keeping current on technical skills. As a college student I took a class on photography and learned all about the chemical processes for developing film and printing pictures to create a valued product—a preserved memory. The valued product of photography hasn't changed, but the process has. If Ansel Adams were living in today's high-tech world, my guess is he'd still be a photographer, but he'd be a master of the digital process—and perhaps the chemical process, as well.

We can also create value in relationships, and one of the best ways we do that is through encouragement. It isn't enough to *notice* if someone is doing well or in need of support; the value comes when we *notify* him or her of our appreciation or our help.

This focus on value provides powerful ways to apply timeless truths to present and future challenges, and that will sustain you in an Up, Down, and Sideways world.

CHAPTER 7

CREATE AND KEEP CONNECTIONS

Take care of the relationships that matter.

WHEN I WAS elected president of the National Speakers Association (NSA), John Ashcroft offered some profound words of wisdom. When you are a leader, he said, many will befriend you, but only a few will be your friend.

John, a former US senator, former governor of Missouri, and former US attorney general, spoke from experience. And, of course, he spoke the truth.

As a longtime member of the NSA, I had many close friends throughout the organization. But when I came into the presidential position, I suddenly had a few friends I never knew I had. Why? I could give these new "friends" the best committee assignments. I could recommend them for the main stage at events. I could raise their stars and their stature. But as my term expired, I noticed that many of those friends began befriending the next president, and I rarely if ever heard from them again.

Then there is Marty Grunder.

In 1984 Marty invested twenty-five dollars in a lawn mower he found at a garage sale, and he began cutting grass to save money for college. By 1990, when he was a senior at the University of Dayton (Ohio), Marty's "little" business was grossing more than $300,000 a year. Grunder Landscaping now employs around forty people and has annual sales of more than $4.5 million.

Creating a connection is important but not nearly as important as keeping that connection.

Marty's success as an entrepreneur got the attention of other entrepreneurs and business leaders who wanted to learn from his experience, so he began speaking publicly and eventually became a member of the NSA.

We first met at the airport as we were leaving an NSA event. He sought my advice on his speaking career, and we soon developed a professional relationship and a friendship. Marty is great at staying in touch, sending me interesting information, and generally looking out for my welfare. He's always appreciative and encouraging.

I've learned a great deal from my relationship with Marty, but one of the most important things is this: creating a connection is important but not nearly as important as keeping that connection.

LIFE CONNECTED

When life is Up, Down, or Sideways, you want the Marty Grunders of the world by your side. These aren't networkers who say they want to share resources and stay connected but disappear when the transaction ends or when your resources and connections no longer provide them with obvious benefits.

Marty and others like him are the people who hold you accountable when you are Up, jump-start you when you are Sideways, and stick with you when you are Down.

Whether you're dealing with your business, your family, your health, your faith, or any other area of your life, they are there for you.

In his book *It's Not Just Who You Know*, my friend Tommy Spaulding defines five levels of relationships, ranging from the transactional (the first floor) up to the transformational (the fifth-floor penthouse). We all have relationships at the five different levels, and most of us, with a little more intentional effort, can have more relationships at higher levels.

Nurturing our relationships, no matter what level they fall into, is a vital principle in taking advantage of the good times and mitigating the down times of our lives. I call it the Connection Concept: take care of your connections—the people you value and who value you.

CONNECTING THROUGH LOVE AND SERVICE

There are dozens of wonderful ways to view your relationships and potential relationships. Mine is based on the simple concept of input and output. What's coming into your life from other people, and what are you sending out from your life into the lives of other people?

The "other people" are all those you know or come in contact with—your family, your friends, your coworkers, your customers and clients, your community, your waitress at the diner . . . everyone. When you produce something of value, others benefit. Who are those people? And who are the people who impact the value you create?

You don't treat all these people the same, of course. You probably won't ask the waitress at the diner for advice on a career opportunity (although you might), and you probably won't ask your boss for advice on your love life (although you might). Each relationship is unique. But two interconnected concepts are foundational to managing any relationship: love and service.

When you put those two things into your relationships, they will come right back out, but in this case two plus two doesn't equal four; it equals something much more, because you've created a loyalty that becomes a multiplier.

SERVING ABOVE SELF

You've probably heard it said that everyone in every organization is in sales. But selling doesn't create a customer.

Selling creates a transaction. Service—how we treat and care for that person—creates a customer. Without the customer, all is lost. Remember: no customers, no profit. Know customers, know profit. So making a connection with the customer becomes vital to the initial transaction and, more important, to the continued loyalty to your organization or brand.

Likewise, service sets the foundation for all your other relationships. How are you serving your spouse? Your children? Your friends? Your employees? Your boss? Your board of directors? Your church? Your community?

As you process your service to others, keep in mind two things.

1. **Know those you serve.** Know what they value. Understand their scoring systems. For instance, how is your boss scoring your work performance? And how are your customers scoring your product?

When I work with clients on customer-service challenges, there are three questions I tell them to ask their customers: What do you like most about doing business with us? What do you like least? And what do you tell others about our company? You can repurpose those questions for most of your relationships to help you assess the needs and expectations of the people you are serving.

But don't stop there. Keep learning as much as you can about the people you are serving and the people who serve you. This requires moving beyond small talk to the deeper issues in people's lives. Challenging ourselves to really know people is unusual in our culture. It's far too easy to judge people by how they look or act rather than doing the hard work of understanding why. But you can't fully serve people you don't fully understand.

If you can't do it with love, why do it at all?

Few organizations live this better than H-E-B Grocery, the Texas-based chain with more than three hundred stores that's known for its superior service. The chain prides itself on creating a culture of "restless dissatisfaction" and a drive for thinking like its shoppers.

Managers in the Rio Grande Valley, for instance, once noticed an annual spike in the sales of rubbing alcohol. They didn't just increase their stock during that time of the year; they figured out the reason for the spike: customers who couldn't afford air-conditioning used the alcohol to

cool their skin. That led H-E-B to partner with manufactur-
ers to create its own brand of rubbing alcohol that included
moisturizers so that it wouldn't dry out the customers' skin.
The product soon made up 25 percent of H-E-B's rubbing
alcohol sales.

2. Make it about them. The Rotarians have a great
motto: "Service above self." It's an ideal each of us should
adopt in all our relationships. We need to look at others and
put their needs above our own—in personal relationships
as well as business relationships. As Philippians 2:3 puts it,
"In humility value others above yourselves."

I recall being on a panel with Alan Weiss, a fellow
speaker and consultant, when he said, "At the end of the
day, it's about improving people's condition. You make
their situation better." He was talking mainly about customers, but the point transcends customers and applies to
any relationship connection.

If you think you are serving people (your spouse, your
boss, your coworkers, your friends) and they don't feel like
they're being served, then you need to adjust your service to
their situation. Get to know what they really need, and put
their needs ahead of your own. And do it not out of hope

for gain but because it is the right thing to do. Whether you benefit from it is secondary.

YOU CAN'T DO IT WITHOUT LOVE

One of my previous books tells the story of an extraordinary individual who loves his work. My editor at the time deleted the word *love* every place I used it, suggesting instead the phrase "generosity of spirit."

"Why not love?" I asked.

"Because the word *love* freaks businesspeople out," he responded.

I think he was half-right. The word *love* freaks most people out, especially when it's applied to the workplace. More often than not, it is associated with sugary-sweet emotion or sentimentality. "I love my colleagues." "I love my customers." "I love the daily grind." Hollow. Superficial. Cliché.

None of us love every aspect of our jobs because there are no perfect jobs in this imperfect world. But it is possible to love the work we perform, love the people we work with, and love the people we ultimately serve.

And we can do it without going over the top or becoming saccharine.

I saw a great example of this principle lived out during my stay at the Ritz-Carlton in downtown Atlanta. It's a top-of-the-line hotel where everyone on staff provides exceptional service with an attitude of "ladies and gentlemen serving ladies and gentlemen."

One morning I went through the buffet line in the restaurant and ordered an egg-white omelet with lots of vegetables, ham, and a little cheese. "You've got to add a little cheese to an egg-white omelet," I told Jeremy, the chef preparing the omelets. "Otherwise it's just too boring."

For love to make any difference, it needs to be demonstrated and not simply felt; it needs to be both attitude and action.

"Not my omelets!" he boomed. "They're never boring. That's because I add a special ingredient." He paused for effect. "I make my omelets with loooove!"

His unorthodox pronouncement got my attention, but I smiled politely and took the plate to a table. With one bite,

I could tell that Jeremy had created an extraordinary dish for me. A few moments later he came by to see how I liked it. I told him it was terrific, probably because it was made with loooove! Jeremy then got serious for a moment. "If you can't do it with love," he said, "why do it at all?"

Chef Jeremy gets it. He understands that when we allow love to define who we are as we work, we become irresistible leaders with a contagious passion for what we do. We are taking care of the people who benefit from the value we produce and nurturing the relationships that impact our value.

THE INGREDIENTS OF LOVE

To make love a part of our value and a driving force in how we nurture our connections, we must begin by reorienting our conventional understanding of the term. For the purposes of this book, I define love as finding a deep-seated passion for what we do, the people we do it with, and the people we do it for. Regardless of the type of work we do, we can find fulfillment and meaning in at least one of these areas.

For love to make any difference, it needs to be demonstrated and not simply felt; it needs to be both attitude and action. One important way is through service, which we've already explored. Here are a few additional ways to make it happen:

Patience. Love is choosing to accept someone—imperfections, weaknesses, demands, and all—regardless of his or her circumstances or needs. We need to meet our connections where they are, not where we want them to be. Patience requires us to set our own expectations aside without indulging in frustration or negativity.

Motivation. Love is patient, but it's not content to leave others where they are. Love does more than focus on what is; it focuses on what could be. Ralph Waldo Emerson once said, "Our chief want is someone who will inspire us to be what we know we could be." Not surprisingly, recognizing a person's potential often starts him or her toward achieving that potential.

Appreciation. Appreciation comes from looking for what's right rather than being hypersensitive to what's wrong. It is about choosing to focus on the positive even when you can't ignore the negative. Too often we forget to stop and express our appreciation to the people who serve alongside us and the people who serve us. From the smallest gesture to the largest bonus or award, people need to know that their work matters. Our customers and coworkers will respond positively every time we offer genuine appreciation . . . guaranteed.

Counsel. Don't tell people what they want to hear. Tell them what they need to hear. Just make sure you tell them in a way that they will listen!

Love means offering wise and insightful advice that is in the best interest of the receiver rather than the giver. Thoughtful input shows that we value the individual and care about his or her needs.

Instruction. Counsel is about the advice we give, while instruction is about teaching someone else with gentleness, discernment, and selflessness. It's one thing for me to give you my opinion, but it takes a commitment of time for me to show you how to implement these suggestions. By offering our experience and hard-won knowledge, we can help others avoid mistakes that we've made, achieve results that we've been able to achieve, and improve beyond what we've been able to accomplish. The most effective teachers walk alongside their students as they learn, appreciating their accomplishments rather than emphasizing their shortcomings.

Time. In our lightning-fast world, where the average attention span is less than two minutes, time is a valuable commodity and should be handled as such. By giving the gift of our time to our connections, we show that we value them above the other things that cry out for our attention.

One of the most powerful love practices at work is the pause—making time to be fully present with another person. We ask each other, "How are you doing?" all the time and never really mean it. How tragic!

Take the time. No, *give* the time.

Compassion. How we do our work makes all the difference. And acting out of compassion is the difference between the mundane and the memorable.

As professionals, we tend to carefully cultivate a slick, confident veneer. But in truth, we are all broken, hurting, wounded people. That's life. My pal, author and speaker Ken Davis, encapsulates our situation well: "I'm not okay, you're not okay, and that's okay."

Acknowledging our weaknesses, mourning our losses,

and comforting each other through difficult times will strengthen our relationships like nothing else can. True compassion requires us to be vulnerable and to admit our own struggles even as we offer empathy and support to others.

Encouragement. Love is offering heartfelt words of affirmation, inspiration, and motivation to the people in our lives. We all need someone—not something—to root for us from the sidelines of our lives. We should seek to notice when others do well and hold them up when they fail. Though often neglected, encouragement is probably the easiest way to incorporate love into our lives and relationships. If we just look around, opportunities to build others up are everywhere.

So how are you doing with love? One method I use to assess myself in this area is to plug my name into a familiar passage from the Bible—1 Corinthians 13:4-7. It says, "Love is patient, love is kind. It does not envy, it does not boast, it is not proud. It does not dishonor others, it is not self-seeking, it is not easily angered, it keeps no record of wrongs. Love does not delight in evil but rejoices with the truth. It always protects, always trusts, always hopes, always perseveres."

Replace the word *love* (and the pronouns that represent it) with your name, and if you're like me, it will convict you and challenge you.

•   •   •

When we create value and deliver it with service and love, we develop connections that increase our value to others, and we multiply their impact on our value. Our products and services become more attractive. We generate better customer response. We develop greater employee retention. And we build meaningful, solid, trustworthy relationships. Best of all, the results invariably lead to a sense of personal fulfillment and renewed motivation that will guide us in our journeys, no matter what circumstances life throws at us.

CHAPTER 8

CONTINUOUSLY INNOVATE

Your competition is always getting better.
Are you?

WOODY HAYES SPENT twenty-eight seasons as the head football coach at Ohio State University, and then he was fired after a now-infamous incident in the 1978 Gator Bowl.

With time running down in the fourth quarter and the Buckeyes already in position to attempt a game-winning field goal, Hayes called a pass play. A Clemson player intercepted the pass and was knocked out of bounds along the Ohio State sideline, securing the victory for the Tigers.

Frustrated by the play and the opponent's celebration, Hayes lost his temper and hit the Clemson player.

For most Ohio State fans, however, that's not the legacy of Woody Hayes. Naturally, some see his legacy in his coaching record—238 wins, 72 losses, 10 ties, 3 national championships, and 13 Big Ten titles. That proved more than enough to land Hayes in college football's Hall of Fame. And Ohio State's Woody Hayes Athletic Center is named in his honor.

Others, however, see his legacy in a chair—the Wayne Woodrow Hayes Chair in National Security Studies. In keeping with his wishes, dona-

Status quo is a myth.   tions made in his honor following his death in 1987 were directed toward academics, which led to the creation of the chair. Hayes, who once grilled Richard Nixon about foreign policy, always took academics as seriously as he did football.

I remember Hayes for all those things, but most of all for something he said during a pep rally when I was a student on the Columbus, Ohio, campus: "Either you're getting better or you're getting worse," he told the crowd. "Status quo is a myth."

I used to think that was coach talk, but time and experience have taught me the truth of what he meant. In a competitive world, if you stay the same, you get passed by. Thus the importance of continuously innovating: you must keep getting better because your competition keeps getting better.

Regardless of whether your personal economy is Up, Down, or Sideways, you can't afford to stay the same. That's because status quo is a myth.

BEST, BETTER, NEXT

Clients often ask me to speak about best practices, and here's what I tell them: I don't believe in best practices.

The phrase *best practices* sounds grand and worthwhile. But the truth is, the concept of best practices always needs a qualifier—best practices . . . for now . . . that we know of . . . given the current circumstances. . . .

Striving for the best has helped many organizations improve. But today's best practices are next week's second-best practices and next month's obsolete practices.

Not only that, but the competition is aware of and likely

practicing the same best practices as you. If they aren't, they soon will be. As advertising guru Lee Clow put it, "When reviewing a list of best practices, keep in mind that someone somewhere is selling them in a book." So if everyone's using the same best practices, that won't give you much of a competitive advantage.

Rather than best practices, I believe in *better* practices and *next* practices.

Better practices: how can we do what everybody else is doing best, but do it better?

Next practices: how can we change the game?

In the home video industry, Blockbuster was best practices. Netflix was better practices. Apple TV is next practices. And as quickly as the world changes, there will probably be a new contender for the throne of next practices by the time you read this book.

Gary Hamel and C. K. Prahalad, in their book *Competing for the Future*, use the labels rule-makers, rule-takers, and rule-breakers. The rule-makers establish strategies within an industry (Cisco, IBM, HP). Rule-takers play by the rules of the rule-makers. Strategy is largely a "positioning exercise." Rule-breakers change the game. They are the upstarts, even if they've been around for years (Apple, Google, Microsoft).

I'm using corporations as the examples here, but this idea applies to each of us as individuals as well. Rule-takers can do okay when times are Up and might survive when times are Sideways, but they lose their place at the table when things are Down. It's not enough to be as good as everybody else. You have to develop the ability to deliver value consistently and to anticipate what your value is going to be in the future. You have to look at what's next. And you have to distinguish yourself from those who are happily focusing on best practices.

MAKE YOUR VALUE DISTINCTIVE

If you think of value as an equation, it would look like this: $V = E + E + SE$, or Value equals Expectations plus Education plus Something Extra. The question facing most of us—and our organizations—is, What's our something extra? What's our distinctive?

Consider the following organizations that go beyond what's expected:

- The fried pickles at Freshcraft, a Denver restaurant that bills itself as "upscale comfort food in a casual atmosphere," are dyed red just to make them different.

- On Super Bowl Sunday one year, the pastor at the church I attend preached on why Christianity is like the Super Bowl. The ushers and staff wore football jerseys, and the congregation batted a beach ball around while singing praise songs.

- At Fiesta Americana resorts in Mexico, the groundskeepers establish eye contact with the guests and greet them in Spanish. "When our guests come to Mexico," the general manager told me, "they want an authentic experience. So we encourage our groundskeepers to say hello in Spanish and even teach the guests a few words in Spanish if time allows."

- *SUCCESS* magazine includes an audio CD in each issue. When I asked publisher Darren Hardy why he didn't just use a link to an audio stream, he wisely pointed out that that's what everybody else is doing. Even though the hard CD costs more to include, it is a distinctive value addition for subscribers.

I have a file folder full of similar examples of products and services that qualify as innovative, and not just because of some technological breakthrough. In fact, when you really think about innovation, it's not as much about the invention of something new as it is about the distinction of something—new or old. I'll go so far as to say the purpose of innovation is distinction. And distinction is found in what you do, how you do it, the product you offer, the service you provide, and the experiences you create.

It's not enough to be different. Being different without being valued is being weird. Distinction is being different *and* valued. So make your value distinctive.

THE PIANO EFFECT

Robert Bloom, the former CEO of Publicis Worldwide, clearly remembers why his father almost always stopped at Mobil stations for gas when the family was traveling around the country: clean restrooms.

That value created a "preference," as Bloom calls it.

"You create preference by giving your customers small—or big—benefits," Bloom said in a 2011 interview with *SUCCESS* magazine. "You don't have to give away the store. There are a lot of ways to create top-of-mind awareness and preference."

I was in a mall in Oak Brook, Illinois, during the Christmas shopping season when something grabbed my attention and created a preference. In the center of Nordstrom, the high-end department store, a man sat on a bench and played holiday music on a baby grand piano. His tunes floated through the air, mixing among the racks of clothes and the displays of jewelry and providing warmth to the shopping atmosphere.

As I made my way through the rest of the mall, the other stores were decked out in reds and greens. I spent time in four other stores, all decorated pretty much the same and all with one other thing in common: no piano player. Nordstrom had successfully created what I now call the Piano Effect—that thing so different and valued about your work or business that when customers go elsewhere, they notice its absence and return to you.

As we innovate—personally and at an organizational level—we do well to ask ourselves this question: what am I doing to create a Piano Effect?

At least six distinctives add value to anything and thereby create a Piano Effect: more, better, faster, different, less, or "funner."

Your **more** might be more hours of operation, more of your product for the same price, more flavors of ice cream, more locations, more solutions, more legroom in the airplane, or more convenience.

Your **better** involves quality. The restrooms in your gas stations are cleaner. Stanley Marcus, the late president and chairman of the board of Neiman Marcus, liked to say, "Quality is remembered long after price is forgotten." Your quality shines through in your product, your services, your commitment, your presentation, the appearance of your work area—everything you do, say, or sell.

Today's best practices are next week's second-best practices and next month's obsolete practices.

Your **faster** demonstrates how you value the time of the people you are serving. Do you meet deadlines? Do you return phone calls and e-mail in a timely manner? Do you get the package there overnight, the oil changed in ten minutes or less, and the pizza there in less than thirty minutes? Do you add value by getting things done faster than your competition?

Your **different** takes you beyond the ordinary response to any situation to create something of value that gets noticed because it stands out from others. Do you dye your fried pickles red, risk being hokey with a Super Bowl–themed church service, or instruct your groundskeepers to interact with guests?

Or how about this: do you solve problems you didn't create?

I keep a letter in my files from a traveler who had a problem with America West Airlines some years ago. He wrote to the president of that airline, but he also sent a copy to Herb Kelleher, who at that time was president of Southwest Airlines.

America West responded with a form letter that said something like, "Sorry you had a problem," but they didn't do anything about it. Kelleher's response was along these lines: "We don't say anything negative about our competition, but we're sorry you had a problem. If you'd like to try Southwest in the future, here's a voucher good for a flight anywhere we go in the country." Herb solved a problem he didn't create, and for thirty-nine dollars he bought a customer for life.

Your **less** isn't necessarily the opposite of your more; it's just different. Can you provide the same products for less money, as Wal-Mart promises? Can you save someone time and money, as Soundview Executive Book Summaries promises? Can you provide fewer hassles, less stress, or less of whatever it is the people you value don't want in an experience or product? If you can, you create a distinctive that lasts.

Your **"funner"** is all about the experiences you create. I know, *funner* isn't a word. But it should be, because it represents a really important ideal in creating value and it rolls off the lips with more, well, *fun* than "more fun." Ever eat at restaurants where the waiter tosses you the rolls or where it's okay to put peanut shells on the floor? That's different, sure, but the difference is the element of fun. It's like the flight attendant who adds some humor to the normally dull, same-old talk you get every time you fly.

A friend and his wife went to a Chick-fil-A expecting nothing more than the usual quick but good chicken sandwich. They didn't realize it was Valentine's Day weekend until they were greeted at the door in French and walked into a restaurant decorated to resemble Paris. A string quartet was playing music, and two employees were giving away free desserts. Everyone in the place, including the people wearing cow costumes, was having fun. What could have been a routine meal at a quick-serve restaurant became something much, much more. It was "funner."

● ● ●

Spillers Records faced perhaps the biggest challenge in its iconic history during the summer of 2010. With its rent on the rise, its industry in a free fall, and the economy limping along somewhere in between, it looked like the time had finally come to pull the plug on the turntables.

The world's oldest record store, founded in 1894 by Henry Spiller, had been at the same location in Cardiff, Wales, for sixty years, but area revitalization projects had changed the neighborhood landscape. With the high-end makeover came higher rents, and Spillers had barely survived a rent increase five years earlier.

This time, owner Nick Todd decided to move the store to a new location with lower overhead costs. He then handed control of the business to his two daughters, ages twenty-seven and thirty-one, respectively, in hopes that the new-generation owners could keep its discs spinning.

How can a century-old store survive in an industry that once was Up, has often been Sideways, and now—and for the foreseeable future—is Down? By acting on the Innovation Imperative and creating its own Piano Effect—a value-based distinction that provides something more, better, faster, different, less, or "funner."

Shortly after the store relocated, Ashli Todd, the store's co-owner and manager, told a blogger what she sees as the Spillers distinctive. "A physical record shop really has to be the antithesis of your one-stop click online—a shop where you want to lose three hours of your life," she said. "It doesn't have to just be about buying a record. It should be a comfortable space, a happy environment, where people can look through magazines or check out gig listings. And recommendations are a really big part. You build a relationship with customers. We get to know what they want and then we can say, 'Hey, we think you'll like this. Have a listen.' That enthusiasm has kept us where we are for so long."

If Spillers can create the types of more, better, faster, different, less, or "funner" that people want, then it will survive. If not, it won't. No best practices can save it. Only better practices and next practices. Spillers' competition and customer base won't stop changing, so Spillers must respond. As Woody Hayes might tell them—and you—there is no status quo.

CHAPTER 9

BUILD RESERVES

Use the Survivor's Secret.

MY SECOND COUSIN Lew Sanborn injured his shoulder in 1956 while in France training for an international sky-diving competition. This was well before the development of deployment bags and sleeves that reduce the shock that comes when a parachute unpacks, unfolds, grabs the air, and turns a free fall into a float. So when he arrived in Moscow, the site of the competition, Lew made some self-designed modifications to his suspension lines in an effort to reduce the jerk he would feel on his ailing shoulder.

His practice jump—jump number ninety-nine in what would be a Hall of Fame skydiving career—went fine, as did his first three jumps in the competition. But there was a problem on career jump number 103.

"I had a streamer on the main canopy in a world competition," Lew says. "That was really embarrassing."

A streamer occurs when the main chute doesn't open properly, leaving the canopy whistling in the wind. It's not only embarrassing but also potentially deadly because the failed chute provides little resistance and therefore doesn't help much to slow the skydiver's fall. So Lew had to cut away the main chute and deploy his backup in order to land safely.

Lew, who would become the first licensed professional skydiver in the United States, now has more than seven thousand jumps to his credit. We talked as he was preparing for his eighty-first birthday and planning his next jumps. Just like on that day in 1956, his plans included a backup chute.

"I'd never jump without one," he said. "I wouldn't even consider it unless it was an emergency."

Skydivers employ a backup chute roughly once in every

one thousand jumps, and even more frequently if they are using a parachute with a smaller canopy. Lew has needed his half a dozen times.

Statistical probability doesn't help skydivers like Lew predict, and thus avoid, a bad chute. They don't know if that one in a thousand will come on their first jump or on their one-thousandth jump or somewhere in between. Despite the many safety innovations in skydiving through the years, every jump involves risk. That's why every skydiver jumps with a backup chute. You can think of it as the Survivor's Secret: you protect what you value by building reserves.

THE ECONOMICS OF RESERVES

Jack LaLanne, known as "the Godfather of Fitness" for his innovative and passionate promotion of healthy diet and exercise, held some interesting views on participating in the pleasures of life: he was all for them, even the ones that weren't so good for you.

Drinking? Staying out all night at parties or clubs? Such vices were okay with LaLanne—but only for those who had paid the price. That price wasn't monetary, but physical. LaLanne, who died in 2011 at the age of ninety-six, preached against overindulgence, but surprisingly not abstinence from things that aren't good for the body. How did he rationalize such seemingly contradictory views?

"They've earned the right," LaLanne said in an interview on the eve of his seventieth birthday. "It's just like . . . if you write a check for one thousand dollars but have only five hundred dollars in the bank, you're bankrupt. But if you have five thousand dollars in the bank, you can afford it. . . . What you put into life you can take out."

I wouldn't take the point to LaLanne's extreme. As the saying goes, just because you *can* do something doesn't mean you *should*. Plus, he was commenting on the physical rather than the moral aspects of such behaviors. But as an economist, I find his approach pretty basic. In fact, it squares perfectly with the things Francis McCormick taught us in his entry-level economics class at Ohio State. Economics, he told us, is about the allocation of resources. A little saved or developed regularly equals a lot available consistently. When you build up your resources, you can then take them out and spend them on whatever you want.

McCormick went on to explain the allocation of resources as units called *utils* (in economics, a measure of utility). To understand utils, he said, assume you have four dollars. The beer at Lefty's Bar is two dollars a pint. The beer at the Oar House is one dollar a pint. Your utils at Lefty's are two, and your utils are four at the Oar House.

This, I thought, *is useful information.*

That's also when I realized that economics is about life. We only have so much time, energy, money, and expertise. We decide how we will allocate those resources—to our benefit or to our loss, as well as to the benefit or loss of others. And the more we have, the more we can draw on—for self-focused pleasure, as LaLanne pointed out; for noble activities, such as helping our friends, families, and communities; or for emergencies, as with backup parachutes.

WHERE TO BUILD OUR RESERVES

Everybody wants to thrive, but we can't thrive if we don't survive. And we won't survive if we don't build reserves to protect the things we value.

We do this, for starters, by keeping our pipelines full

of important relationships, valuable projects, and potential customers, as we covered in chapter 6. That's part of creating value that puts us in a position to succeed, regardless of the circumstances around us. But to protect that value when the main chute doesn't open, we'd better have something in reserve.

The four main areas in which we all need reserves are financial, physical, psychological, and spiritual.

These are what I call quasi-limited resources. Some resources—time, for instance—are fixed. We all have the same twenty-four hours in each day. We can increase our efficiency with that time, but we can't increase the time itself.

The best financial advice you or I will ever get is still this: spend less than you make.

Other resources have limits, but we seldom test those limits. There's a limit to how much weight I can bench-press, but I could change that limit if I spent more time lifting weights and developing my muscles. I'll probably never discover the ultimate limit to my bench-pressing abilities, however, because I'll never push myself that far.

Our limits are important because they shape how much we can put in our reserves. It's up to each of us to grow our resources and figure out how we allocate them—how much we use each day and how much we put in reserve.

Financial Reserves

Here are some statistics that seem disconcerting, if not frightening, to me. According to a 2011 study by the Employee Benefit Research Institute, 29 percent of workers say they have less than $1,000 in savings and investments, while 56 percent say their savings and investments, excluding the value of their homes, total less than $25,000.

In other words, they have little or no financial reserves.

The best financial advice you or I will ever get is still this: spend less than you make. The rationale is simple: we only need financial savings when times are bad, and when times are bad, we can't create them. Thus, we have to create them when times are Up or Sideways. Yet most Americans don't practice this basic tenet of finance.

I believe saving is something we should do regardless of our circumstances. There might be times when we can't save as much, but anything we put back is more than putting nothing back. Maybe you've heard a story similar to this one about the sixty-year-old guy who argued against taking Spanish language classes because, he reasoned, it would take him ten years to learn the language.

"By then," he said, "I'll be seventy."

"That's right," he was told. "But if you don't take lessons, you still won't be able to speak Spanish when you're seventy."

Changing our spending and saving habits isn't easy, especially in a culture of consumerism that makes buying a hobby. But it is possible. Building financial reserves starts with a commitment to do so, and it's never too late to start.

If you're looking for a place to begin, make a list of everything you spent the last few months. Create a budget that includes tactics and strategies for paying off debt and saving money. Take a course on financial management. Enlist the support of the people around you—you'll need their accountability and encouragement, and they can celebrate with you as you pass certain milestones and begin building reserves.

Physical Reserves

You can raise all sorts of moral questions about Jack LaLanne's views, but practically speaking, it's hard to argue with his central point. Building physical reserves through diet and exercise mitigates the negative attacks on your body. You'll offset them even more, I would argue, the less you take part in self-focused and self-destructive behaviors. I'd also argue that many effects from the self-destructive behaviors take years to surface, so it's easy to develop a false sense of security.

But I do agree that taking care of yourself physically allows you to grow some much-needed reserves. You get sick less often. You feel better in general. You think more clearly. If something happens beyond your control—my cancer, for instance—you're better prepared to handle it and bounce back more quickly. And while I'd recommend avoiding all-night parties, drugs, and binge drinking, building some physical reserves gives you the freedom to indulge in an occasional donut, dessert, or other guilty pleasure. I've found that indulgences become detrimental when they go from occasional to regular, and the distance between the two is a slippery slope. I've learned to set limits on such indulgences, like eating red meat only twice a week.

Not only that, but study after study supports the mental benefits of exercise. In a report published on Fitness.gov, Arizona State University's Dr. Daniel Landers concluded, "There is now ample evidence that a definite relationship exists between exercise and improved mental health. This is particularly evident in the case of a reduction of anxiety and depression. For these topics, there is now consider-able evidence derived from over hundreds of studies with thousands of subjects to support the claim that 'exercise is related to a relief in symptoms of depression and anxiety.'"

Psychological Reserves

We can inherit a fortune or win big in the lottery, but we can't build our psychological reserves in an instant; we have to build them gradually over time. More and more evi-dence suggests that factors such as exercise, diet, rest, and strong relational support networks are contributing factors to psychological health—even more important than medi-cations or therapy for most people.

Studies of autopsies on the elderly show that as many

as two-thirds of them die with Alzheimer's disease, many with advanced cases, even though they showed few signs of the disease when they were alive. Scientists attribute this to "cognitive reserves"—the brain's ability to develop and maintain extra neurons and keep them connected.

Such reserves are built and strengthened in many ways, starting with activities that challenge the intellect. That's why it's so important to continue learning and reading good books. And who knew we could classify the crossword or sudoku puzzle as preventative medicine?

A strong relational network also challenges us, encourages us, and provides support. Diet and exercise keep us physically fit so we can fuel our minds properly. And rest helps us think more clearly.

I once heard weariness defined as the exhaustion of pleasure. We avoid weariness by getting the necessary rest we need to stay motivated. If you eat right and exercise, rest comes more easily. Of course, the stresses of life can keep all of us up at night, so we can face a somewhat circular challenge: we need more rest to reduce our stress, but stress is making it hard to rest.

There's no easy answer to this. But I'm convinced we

can prepare for stress and anxiety the same way we take on other challenges: by working our way toward increased resistance. In other words, practice releasing stress when it comes to little things, and over time it becomes easier to release it on the bigger things. Pick a minor annoyance, and consciously give up the thought immediately. Releasing little frustrations helps us deal with the bigger ones.

Shawn Achor, author of *The Happiness Advantage*, refers to this as "the Zorro Circle." He argues that we can regain control of overwhelming emotions by training our brains to focus "first on small, manageable goals, and then gradually expanding our circle to achieve bigger and bigger ones."

Spiritual Reserves

Most people would agree there is a spiritual dimension to life that directly affects how we define success.

Pollster George Gallup Jr. backs up this idea. "The deeper you go with faith," he says in an interview with *Life@Work*, "the more it has an effect in very measurable ways on society in terms of a better outlook, healthier lifestyles, a higher feeling of self-esteem, love of self and love of others. We can document that right and left."

By practicing the disciplines of your faith—prayer, reading, theological study, etc.—you can build the reserves that give you peace in the storms. I've found that making time each morning to read, think, and pray provides a positive foundation for my day ahead.

Dallas Willard, a philosophy professor at the University of Southern California, puts it this way in *Renovation of the Heart*: "A carefully cultivated heart will, assisted by the grace of God, foresee, forestall, or transform most of the painful situations before which others stand like helpless children saying 'Why?'"

> *Practice releasing stress when it comes to little things, and over time it becomes easier to release it on the bigger things.*

• • •

We need reserves that will sustain us in good times and bad (and all the situations in between). They are essential not only to our success but also to our survival. It is too late to add a backup chute once you've left the plane. Building financial, physical, spiritual, and psychological reserves takes effort, but when this is done consistently, it gives us the means to survive virtually any setback.

CHAPTER 10

PRACTICE GRATITUDE

Discover the antidote to negative thinking.

JOHN KRALIK CAME up with a simple plan to shake free
from the melancholy that gripped his life. At fifty-two, he
was a living expression of "Whatever can go wrong will
go wrong." He had gone through his second divorce. His
business was failing, and his finances were crumbling.
His older children were distant, and his relationship with
his younger daughter was shaky. He lived in a small, drafty

apartment. He was forty pounds overweight. And his girl-friend had broken up with him.

What turned things around for him?

Gratitude.

First, he was grateful for a note he received from his ex-girlfriend thanking him for his Christmas present. Second, that gratitude inspired him to change his focus in life from the things he had lost to the things he had and to put that new focus into action by writing thank-you notes. In fact, he decided to write 365 thank-you notes—one per day for a year. Executing that simple action plan, as he explains in the book *365 Thank Yous*, changed his life.

The more grateful you are, the more grace you extend. The more grace you extend, the more grateful you become.

Kralik claims that, while deeply contemplating his situation, he had an epiphany of sorts when he heard a voice say, "Until you learn to be grateful for the things you have, you will not receive the things you want."

THE ACTION OF GRATITUDE

It's easy—and perhaps commonplace—to view gratitude as a feeling. But as Kralik discovered, it's something more than that. It's an emotional *response*. Therefore, it's something we *do*, not just something we *are*.

Gratitude is a feeling accompanied by an action—sometimes an immediate, emotion-driven action and sometimes a strategic course of action borne from reflective thinking and the counsel of others. So if someone pulls us from a burning building, we might shower that person with gratitude. If we strategically give our time, money, and energy to charity, it's most often out of gratitude for that charity's work, for a person working there, and/or for specific results that the charity produces. And sometimes we give simply because we realize how much we've been given. The story of the widow's mite in the Gospel of Luke is a familiar one that demonstrates we all have something to give, regardless of how much or how little we have.

It's the same on a personal level. A friend's daughter is a pediatric neonatal intensive care unit nurse. In other words, she cares for premature babies who often enter the world very, very sick.

It's not unusual for parents of those children to find some way to express their gratitude for the care she provides their newborn children—flowers, thank-you notes, etc. The parents stay in touch, sometimes for years, and they never stop feeling or expressing their gratefulness. When the young nurse moved from an apartment into her first house, one couple gave her a lawn mower and another gave her a leaf blower. Later, a grateful couple set her up on a blind date—with the man she eventually married!

When parents react that way, guess what happens to the nurse? She experiences gratitude herself. She's thankful for her coworkers, for the doctors, for her training, and for the parents' support and appreciation. Plus, she got a lawn mower and a leaf blower . . . and a husband to operate them!

We all have a long list of reasons to express gratitude. For me, it starts with faith, family, and friends—the things I value most in life. We can appreciate the value of the people on our teams and others we interact with at work. We can appreciate the opportunities that come our way. And we can even appreciate the lessons we learn from the trials of life.

The actions we take in response to our gratitude are, in fact, a part of gratitude. It's the virtuous cycle of giving that comes from our thankfulness for the things in life we value. Practice gratitude to maintain your perspective and guide your focus.

GRATITUDE AND GRACE

Roger Scruton, a British philosopher and writer, sees a shift in the meaning and significance of gratitude. He says that rather than teaching, promoting, and regularly expressing genuine gratitude in our daily lives, we all too often limit gratitude to "special occasions, when some individual makes a point of stepping in to help."

As governments have taken over the functions once carried out by charities, Scruton writes in an essay for *The American Spectator*, the idea of justice has replaced the idea of charity. Benefits are handed out equally rather than given as gifts to those in need. It hasn't taken long for gifts to turn into "rights" and for claims to replace gratitude. People express far less gratitude for what they believe is rightly and justly theirs. They are less likely to see anything and everything they get as a result of grace—an unmerited gift.

Grace and gratitude go hand in glove. Grace feeds gratitude, and gratitude fuels grace. The more grateful you are, the more grace you extend. The more grace you extend, the more grateful you become. Gratefulness creates "great fullness" of heart, which produces graciousness.

It's the lack of this quality that prevents far too many people from experiencing success in life. Wealthy, poor, or somewhere in between, there is no peace and no joy—and thus no success—without grace and gratitude.

The chronically thankless are never satisfied.

The chronically dissatisfied are never thankful.

The reverse also holds true.

The chronically thankful are always satisfied.

The chronically satisfied are always thankful.

That's why practicing gratitude is essential to success in the midst of all circumstances. When you are Up, the gift is a reminder not to take your blessings for granted. When you are Down, the gift diminishes your sadness and regrets while raising hope for the future. When you are Sideways, the gift reminds you that gratitude is not situational—it's not dependent on the good times or the bad.

GRATITUDE IS A GIFT

Gratitude in and of itself is a gift.

First, it's the gift of **perspective**. No matter what we've lost, gratitude allows us to focus on what we have. It allows us to focus on what's right, not what's wrong. It literally infects (and affects) our attitude (recall the Optimist's Orientation). Some people think the antidote to negative thinking is positive thinking. It's not. The antidote to negative thinking is gratitude.

Gratitude also keeps us from becoming self-absorbed because it sustains a focus on purposes in life that are greater than ourselves.

Consider two entrepreneurs. One starts a company with the purpose of generating revenue and making a profit so that he can grow his wealth, retire at a young age, and enjoy the fruits of his labor. The other wants to build a company that generates revenue and profit while changing his customers, employees, and the world for the better. One company is built to flip; the other is built to serve. One has a self-focused perspective; the other has an outward-focused perspective. One has an entitlement-based approach to business and life; the other has a gratitude-based approach to business and life.

Second, it's the gift of **energy**. Realizing what we have in life energizes our efforts to do something in response. Expressions of gratitude—notes, gifts, words, acts of service, and the like—refill our tanks. You may not realize it, but gratitude builds up not only other people but also your own psychological and spiritual reserves.

Third, it's the gift of **guidance**. Gratitude reminds us what we value—what is important to us—and where we should focus our time, actions, money, and attention. As you become more conscious of what you're most thankful for, your priorities start to become much clearer.

The antidote to negative thinking is gratitude.

Fourth, it's the gift of **resilience**. I don't know anyone with cancer who will tell you he or she is grateful for the disease. Frankly, that type of happy talk makes little sense. But many people who have cancer or who have survived cancer—or other such challenges in life—will tell you they appreciate what came from the experience. For me the disease was dreadful, but the reminder of my blessings was invigorating. Learning and growing from life's trials is a mature reaction to the things outside of our control.

ACTION-ORIENTED GRATITUDE

The practice of gratitude involves action. What, then, are the actions we can take to develop the practice of gratitude? Here are three simple action steps.

Start with a mind-set of gratitude. Being grateful is a mind-set. When you count your blessings, you think about them. And when you think about them, you act on them, often in ways you never expected. The ancient wisdom in the book of Proverbs still rings true: "As he thinketh in his heart, so is he" (23:7, KJV). Adopt a mind-set of gratitude, and grateful you will be.

My friend Tim Sanders wrote a book called *Today We Are Rich*. The title comes from an experience he had with his grandmother, who said that expression to him after giving some money to someone in need. He was just a kid, but he knew his family wasn't wealthy. So he asked her what she meant when she said they were rich.

"By being able and willing to give," she explained, "we are rich."

Giving is less about how much money you have (recall the widow and her mite) and more about how rich you are in spirit. Grateful people are givers. For them, gratitude isn't just a feeling. Gratitude is a practice, and it's expressed through giving.

Tim, by the way, has a wonderful scoring system for his gratitude. He calls it POET: People, Opportunities, Experiences, Things. He wants to develop a mind-set for gratitude in that order. So, for instance, if a friend gives him a nice watch as a birthday present, his gratitude is first for the giver, not for the timepiece.

Schedule gratitude. With a mind-set of gratitude, you can schedule gratitude. That might sound mechanical or sterile, but it is a way to develop a powerful habit. Put it on your calendar until it becomes second nature. Schedule time each day to make a list of the good things that happened and to write notes to people who were nice to you.

Make it a point to send a thank-you text to a friend or to post a thankful thought on Facebook.

Practice giving as you can. With a mind-set of gratitude, opportunities to give will emerge around you. Don't miss them. You'll probably feel an urge to do something a little off the wall (like taking a homeless person to lunch rather than just giving him or her a little cash). Go ahead and do it. Plan some giving, whether it's your time or your money, but don't ignore opportunities to be an impromptu giver. The benefits will stay with you longer than you can imagine, and they will serve you well regardless of whether times are Up, Down, or Sideways.

CHAPTER 11

EMBRACE DISCIPLINE

Consistently act on your intentions.

SCOTT GINSBURG, a friend and successful corporate speaker and entrepreneur, once asked me a terrific question. "Mark," he said, "what are the three or four things you do every day to grow your business?"

Scott understands a basic tenet for success: it isn't based on what we know, believe, or intend; it's a result of what we consistently do. So in order to maximize the Ups, mitigate the Downs, and push through the Sideways, we have to move beyond good intentions. We need the one critical ingredient that drives the process forward.

We need to embrace discipline as a driver for success.

Discipline is the ability to do what needs to be done even when we don't feel like doing it. It's the connective tissue between our intellectual intent and our behavioral muscle. And the key to developing any behavior, like any muscle, is consistency. Haphazard or inconsistent action is better than none at all, but we benefit most from consistently doing the right things.

Discipline allows us to develop the things we value and set ourselves up for success regardless of the circumstances around us. It puts our good intentions into action, but it's not an all-confining, legalistic doctrine. In other words, it drives our *results,* not our *lives.* Our values, dreams, ambitions, and aspirations should drive our lives. Discipline drives all the processes that create results.

THE DOCTRINE OF DISCIPLINE

On my way to work each morning I see the same woman running the same route. I don't know who she is, but she's there every day, as dependable as the sunrise, putting in her miles.

I can only speculate on her motivation. Maybe she's just staying in shape (building physical reserves). Maybe she's an elite athlete, and this is part of her training regimen. This I do know: she is disciplined. And discipline isn't sexy. It is routine and consistent, like clockwork.

When that same methodical, underappreciated discipline is applied to the mind-sets and methods we've

Success isn't based on what we know, believe, or intend; it's a result of what we consistently do.

talked about in this book, it will drive you toward success. But what does discipline look like? What are some of the things that distinguish this principle and bring light to your values?

Let's look at some ways to understand the art of discipline.

Discipline requires farsighted faith, not blind faith. Discipline is a present investment with the goal of future gains. With blind faith, you move forward with no idea whether your actions will produce the desired results. It's a form of ignorance, and it depends on factors you can't control, like luck. Farsighted faith rests on an understanding of your skill level and of relevant information. It allows you to manage and mitigate risks. It tells you that just because something isn't working now, that doesn't mean it won't work in the future if you stick to it. I'm pretty sure the woman I see running each morning doesn't feel the benefits during every morning run, but at the same time I'm quite certain she knows there are benefits accruing for her health in the future.

Discipline comes from motivation. Motivation is about far more than feeling good about what you're doing (remember, sometimes we don't feel like doing what needs to be done). It is about having motives for action, and those underlying motives must be compelling for us to stay disciplined. While others can inspire us and help us stay motivated, ultimately it is an inside job. You're the only one who can pull yourself out of bed in the morning and do what needs to be done. If you don't have motives behind your actions, then obviously you won't act.

Discipline includes scoring systems for making good decisions. Your actions begin with your decisions, so a core discipline should include processes for consistently making good decisions. Scoring systems like the one you should use to determine your definition of success can work in all sorts of other areas of life, including your decision making.

For instance, I have a system for choosing business opportunities: interesting people, interesting profits, interesting places, or interesting projects. If a project doesn't hit on at least two or three of those things, it probably isn't a great deal for me. In business, of course, profit is paramount, but you can balance it against other things you value. I've turned down projects that could have been profitable because I felt no passion for them or because I didn't share the same value system as the potential client.

Discipline travels the path of *some* resistance. Taking the path of least resistance sounds smart enough, but when you go that route, you develop no muscle or moxie. Things work out easily, but the process doesn't make you better.

The path of some resistance recognizes that challenges develop stamina and skill. If you've done much hiking, you know that some of the best views are found at the end of the most challenging trails.

When you take the path of some resistance, you end up telling someone what he or she needs to hear rather than what that person wants to hear. Or you might choose to do something that requires physical exertion over letting a machine do the work. And it almost always means going beyond yourself in service to others. The path of least resistance counts on "the system" to help those in need. The path of some resistance doesn't mean you can or should help everyone, but it acknowledges the tragedy of helping no one.

The path of some resistance also teaches you not to give up when you hit big resistance. Walt Disney faced several financial setbacks in the 1920s and was $4 million in debt in the early 1930s. But he pulled together just enough financing to cover the production of *Snow White and the Seven Dwarfs*, and that film's success in 1938 not only pulled the Walt Disney Company out of bankruptcy but also financed its new studios.

Some of the best views are found at the end of the most challenging trails.

"You may not realize it when it happens," Disney once

said, "but a kick in the teeth may be the best thing in the world for you."

Discipline puts in the inevitable hard work of success. If it were easy, everyone would do it, right? Being disciplined requires stamina and a willingness to go beyond what most others are willing to do. The best speakers I know are those who are willing to spend more time researching their audiences and preparing their presentations. They labor longer behind the scenes, and the fruits of that labor become apparent when they take the stage.

George Bernard Shaw described it this way: "When I was a young man, I observed that nine out of ten things I did were failures. I didn't want to be a failure, so I did ten times more work."

"MAKE" TIME FOR THE IMPORTANT THINGS

Chapter 2 talks about the barriers that keep us from doing the things we know are important. Why is it that you sometimes know what to do but then don't do it consistently? Because you fail to MAKE time for the things that really matter. MAKE is an acronym I use as a reminder of four ways to free up space to consistently do what's important.

Modify what you do so that you spend less time doing certain activities. You can fill your day checking e-mail and surfing the web for funny pictures or interesting videos. Or you can modify your behavior and stop letting technology own you rather than your owning it.

Adjust your schedule so that high-priority items get done first. You shouldn't just start with the easy. Start with what matters most so that you can make progress on the important things before the routine intrusions get in the way.

Know what is important. Without clear priorities, you'll often invest your time and energy in things that aren't really giving a good return. You need to base your priorities on your values and not what others assign importance to.

Eliminate bad habits. Every unexamined habit carries the potential of becoming a bad habit. You might have started a routine for all the right reasons, but things change with time. Ask yourself, *What would happen if I stopped* *doing this?* The answer will help you decide if you should cut back on it, eliminate it, or improve on it.

THE DAILY DISCIPLINES

Painters create art one brush stroke at a time. Authors compose books one sentence at a time. Masons build cathedrals one brick at a time. What are the brush strokes, the sentences, or the brick foundations of your day? What are your disciplines—the things you do every day to ensure success regardless of whether times are Up, Down, or Sideways?

We've hit on several actionable items in the previous chapters, but here are some of the daily (or at least regular) disciplines needed to succeed when times are good, bad, or in between:

The Scorekeeper's System: Be intentional about choosing and evaluating your scoring system.

The Optimist's Orientation: Start the day expecting the best of yourself and great outcomes from your work.

The Learner's Leverage: Learn something each day, and read something each day.

Produce Value: Create a checklist of the things you provide that others value, as well as the people who value what you provide, and continually evaluate and improve it.

Create and Keep Connections: Make time each day to take care of important connections. As your day comes to a close, make some mental notes of the opportunities you embraced and those you ignored.

Continuously Innovate: Make a list of what could be your *next practices*. Look for ways each day to make your value more, better, faster, different, less, and "funner."

Build Reserves: Make it a priority to exercise your financial, physical, mental, and spiritual muscles every day.

Practice Gratitude: Give one heartfelt compliment or write one thank-you note each day.

CHAPTER 12

CONCLUSION: HOW TO SUCCEED ALL THE TIME

Persistence turns productive behavior into positive habits.

IS IT POSSIBLE to succeed all the time, regardless of your circumstances? My experience suggests that it is. This isn't just a semantic sleight of hand or a play on words. If success is about doing the right things consistently, knowing that we will ultimately benefit from them, then the only real failure is when we quit trying and resign ourselves to our current situation. If success only means having what we want when we want it, no, we can't succeed all the time. But if success is about thriving despite obstacles and setbacks, then success truly is a choice we can make all the time.

As you read the final pages of this book, you likely resonate with one of the three stages—Up, Down, or Sideways. Maybe everything for you is Up. Life is grand. Or perhaps you are Down. You've hit rock bottom in every aspect of life. Or possibly you're stuck in a rut of mediocrity. You are Sideways.

Then again, maybe you're experiencing all three. Maybe you would say something like, "My professional life is Up, but my family life is Down, and my physical condition is Sideways."

The focus of this book has been on the things you should do regardless of the circumstances, but there are also things you might need an extra supply of when you find yourself Up, when you find yourself Down, or when you find yourself Sideways. Keep these in mind as you put the principles of this book into practice and as you share them with others.

When you're Up, you need humility and perspective. Sure, you worked hard and earned your success, but you didn't get Up all by yourself. None of us get there alone.

Other people and often forces outside your control contributed to your rise. Not only that, but you can't take Up for granted. You need to remember that setbacks are inevitable, and they'll come particularly soon if you stop doing the things that got you Up and that mitigate potential trouble.

Surround yourself with people who keep you grounded.

When you're Sideways, you need a boost. Sideways breeds complacency. You are neither hot nor cold. You're *comfortable.* When things are Sideways, there's no big victory to celebrate but also no sense of urgency to make things better. You know you could improve, but you've become satisfied with the status quo and indifferent about change.

Surround yourself with people who challenge you to keep moving in the right direction.

When you're Down, you need hope. The greatest bankruptcy you face in life isn't about finances; it's a loss of hope. The loss of hope doesn't just cripple you and keep you from moving; it keeps you from thinking that moving would make a difference. If you've lost hope, you are in a form of bankruptcy—mental, spiritual, or emotional bankruptcy.

I vividly recall a meeting several years ago with some of my closest colleagues. At the time, my business had grown annually for nearly twenty consecutive years. But one person in the group was struggling with a big business setback, and one of our wisest colleagues offered this counsel: "If you live long enough, you inevitably suffer a setback. When it happens, don't be surprised or discouraged. Life is cyclic. Just keep doing the right things until the cycle ends." A few years later those words encouraged me greatly as I endured my first significant downturn.

Surround yourself with people who lift your spirits.

PERSISTENCE IN PRACTICE

There is one essential ingredient to succeeding when times are Up, Down, or Sideways: persistence. It is an underlying theme throughout this book, because persistence turns productive behavior into positive habits.

So what does this look like?

For me, it looks a lot like Nicholas Maxim.

Nicholas was born with arms that end just above the elbows and legs that end just above the knees. By the time he was ten years old, however, Nicholas had learned to grip a pencil with his arm stubs so he could write. He worked so hard at it, in fact, that he learned to write in cursive. And he learned to write so well that his teachers submitted his writing as an entry into the National Handwriting Contest. The judges were so impressed that they created a special award for students with disabilities and named it after its first recipient—the Nicholas Maxim Special Award for Excellent Penmanship.

Everett Maxim has seen his son struggle through the challenges that come with physical disabilities, and he counts himself among the growing number of fans who are inspired by his son's persistence.

"No matter what it is," Everett says of his son, "if he wants to do something, he puts his mind to it and keeps working on it until he gets it the way he wants it."

What I'm writing about is also personified in one of my closest friends. I spoke with Joel as I was writing this chapter, and he told me he had just lost his job—for the third time in a period of a little more than two years. His job losses have been due not to his performance but to a force bigger than him: the economy in general and his job sector in particular. Joel is a skilled sales professional, a hard worker, and a man of integrity. But once again he's

unemployed and looking for a new way to support his family. My heart broke for my friend. Yet when he shared the
news, it seemed I was far more worried about his future
than he was.

Why no angst or gnashing of teeth? It isn't that he is
indifferent; he is just confident that things will turn out all
right.

Is he delusional? In denial? Overly optimistic?

He is none of those things. He's just persistent. He
knows he will never quit trying. And he knows if he keeps
trying, good things will happen.

Without comparing notes with me, this friend has practiced many of the principles in this book. He's proof that
these principles work. They worked for him when he was at
the top of his career, and they're working for him now as he
deals with a downturn.

You don't know Joel, but hopefully you are very much
like him—someone whose faith and values provide a foundation for dealing with success and handling setbacks. A
person ready for Up, Down, or Sideways. That doesn't mean
that everything will work out perfectly for you, but that

you are the kind of person whose values and persistently applied practices put you in a position to succeed.

That's the secret to living Up, Down, or Sideways.

Acknowledgments

It takes a team to launch a book, so I want to acknowledge the following people and express my gratitude:

Matt Yates and Sealy Yates at Yates & Yates, for their excellent representation. This is our fourth book together, and you are valued colleagues and friends.

Stephen Caldwell, for his assistance and collaboration. You truly helped me sharpen my saw.

Stephanie Voiland, my editor, for her editing skills. I appreciate both your abilities and your concern for my success.

Jon Farrar, Ron Beers, April Kimura-Anderson, and the many other wonderful people at Tyndale who have assisted in so many ways. I hope my wacky sense of humor has added to the process.

To my longtime friend and speaker-colleague Eric Chester, for his insights. You are always a trusted adviser, and you help me maintain my perspective.

To Tim Sanders, who practices what he teaches. Thanks for the great ideas you've shared.

To the readers of my previously released books. I truly hope my work has encouraged and enriched your life and that this book will do the same.

To my wife, Darla, who is my most insightful critic and greatest supporter. Thank you, sweetheart, for helping me pursue my calling.

And finally, but in no way least, to God, the source of all blessings.

About the Author

Mark Sanborn is an internationally acclaimed speaker, a bestselling author, and a noted authority on leadership, customer service, and extraordinary performance. He is the president of Sanborn & Associates Inc., an idea lab for leadership development.

Mark has presented more than 2,400 speeches and seminars in every state and a dozen countries. He holds the Certified Speaking Professional designation from the National Speakers Association and is a member of the Speaker Hall of Fame.

Mark is a past president of the National Speakers Association and a recipient of the Cavett Award, the highest honor bestowed by that organization. In 2007 Mark was awarded the Ambassador of Free Enterprise Award by Sales & Marketing Executives International.

He lives in Highlands Ranch, Colorado, with his wife, Darla, and his sons, Hunter and Jackson.

For more information and resources that complement this book, visit www.marksanborn.com or call 303-683-0714.

Twitter: @mark_sanborn

Facebook: marksanbornspeaker

Learn more about how to succeed when times are good, bad, or in between.

Begin with a Free Audio Lesson

Continue to learn about the methods and mind-sets discussed in this book. We've made the next step as simple and inexpensive as possible—it's free! Visit www.marksanborn.com/UDS to take advantage of these three learning resources: an audio lesson with Mark Sanborn, a summary handout of the key principles in this book, and a subscription to *Leadership Lessons*, Mark's e-newsletter.

Order Learning Resources Today

Mark has created many learning resources, including books, CDs, DVDs, and DVD-based training programs. Learn more about how you and your team can benefit from these resources by visiting www.marksanborn.com/store.

To learn more about live programs at your organization, visit www.marksanborn.com or call 303-683-0714.

Bring Mark Sanborn to Your Organization

Mark Sanborn is an award-winning speaker known for his entertaining and educational presentation style. He provides audiences with actionable ideas and powerful insights on leadership, customer service, and motivation. Having Mark speak can make your next meeting or event extraordinary.

To bring Mark Sanborn to your organization, visit www.marksanborn.com or call 303-683-0714.

CP0508